**INTRODUCING
ISSUES WITH
OPPOSING
VIEWPOINTS®**

Death and Dying

Jacqueline Langwith, *Book Editor*

GREENHAVEN PRESS
A part of Gale, Cengage Learning

GALE
CENGAGE Learning™

Detroit • New York • San Francisco • New Haven, Conn • Waterville, Maine • London

Christine Nasso, *Publisher*
Elizabeth Des Chenes, *Managing Editor*

© 2008 Greenhaven Press, a part of Gale, Cengage Learning

Gale and Greenhaven Press are registered trademarks used herein under license.

For more information, contact:
Greenhaven Press
27500 Drake Rd.
Farmington Hills, MI 48331-3535
Or you can visit our Internet site at gale.cengage.com

For product information and technology assistance, contact us at

Gale Customer Support, 1-800-877-4253
For permission to use material from this text or product, submit all requests online at www.cengage.com/permissions

Further permissions questions can be emailed to permissionrequest@cengage.com

Articles in Greenhaven Press anthologies are often edited for length to meet page requirements. In addition, original titles of these works are changed to clearly present the main thesis and to explicitly indicate the author's opinion. Every effort is made to ensure that Greenhaven Press accurately reflects the original intent of the authors. Every effort has been made to trace the owners of copyrighted material.

Cover image copyright James Steidl, 2007. Used under license from Shutterstock.com

ISBN-13: 978-0-7377-3974-9

Library of Congress Control Number: 2008922580

Printed in the United States of America
2 3 4 5 6 7 12 11 10 09 08

Contents

Chapter 3: What Happens After Death?

Foreword

I
ndulging in a wide spectrum of ideas, beliefs, and perspectives is
a critical cornerstone of democracy. After all, it is often debates
over differences of opinion, such as whether to legalize abortion,
how to treat prisoners, or when to enact the death penalty, that shape
our society and drive it forward. Such diversity of thought is frequent-
ly regarded as the hallmark of a healthy and civilized culture. As the
Reverend Clifford Schutjer of the First Congregational Church in
Mansfield, Ohio, declared in a 2001 sermon, "Surrounding oneself
with only like-minded people, restricting what we listen to or read only
to what we find agreeable is irresponsible. Refusing to entertain doubts
once we make up our minds is a subtle but deadly form of arrogance."
With this advice in mind, Introducing Issues with Opposing Viewpoints
books aim to open readers' minds to the critically divergent views that
comprise our world's most important debates.

Introducing Issues with Opposing Viewpoints simplifies for students
the enormous and often overwhelming mass of material now available
via print and electronic media. Collected in every volume is an array of
opinions that captures the essence of a particular controversy or topic.
Introducing Issues with Opposing Viewpoints books embody the spirit of nineteenth-century journalist Charles A. Dana's axiom: "Fight for
your opinions, but do not believe that they contain the whole truth, or
the only truth." Absorbing such contrasting opinions teaches students
to analyze the strength of an argument and compare it to its opposition. From this process readers can inform and strengthen their own
opinions, or be exposed to new information that will change their minds.
Introducing Issues with Opposing Viewpoints is a mosaic of different
voices. The authors are statesmen, pundits, academics, journalists, cor-
porations, and ordinary people who have felt compelled to share their
experiences and ideas in a public forum. Their words have been collected from newspapers, journals, books, speeches, interviews, and the
Internet, the fastest growing body of opinionated material in the world.

Introducing Issues with Opposing Viewpoints shares many of the well-
known features of its critically acclaimed parent series, Opposing
Viewpoints. The articles are presented in a pro/con format, allowing readers to absorb divergent perspectives side by side. Active reading questions
preface each viewpoint, requiring the student to approach the material

thoughtfully and carefully. Useful charts, graphs, and cartoons supplement each article. A thorough introduction provides readers with crucial background on an issue. An annotated bibliography points the reader toward articles, books, and Web sites that contain additional information on the topic. An appendix of organizations to contact contains a wide variety of charities, nonprofit organizations, political groups, and private enterprises that each hold a position on the issue at hand. Finally, a comprehensive index allows readers to locate content quickly and efficiently.

Introducing Issues with Opposing Viewpoints is also significantly different from Opposing Viewpoints. As the series title implies, its presentation will help introduce students to the concept of opposing viewpoints, and learn to use this material to aid in critical writing and debate. The series' four-color, accessible format makes the books attractive and inviting to readers of all levels. In addition, each viewpoint has been carefully edited to maximize a reader's understanding of the content. Short but thorough viewpoints capture the essence of an argument. A substantial, thought-provoking essay question placed at the end of each viewpoint asks the student to further investigate the issues raised in the viewpoint, compare and contrast two authors' arguments, or consider how one might go about forming an opinion on the topic at hand. Each viewpoint contains sidebars that include at-a-glance information and handy statistics. A Facts About section located in the back of the book further supplies students with relevant facts and figures.

Following in the tradition of the Opposing Viewpoints series, Greenhaven Press continues to provide readers with invaluable exposure to the controversial issues that shape our world. As John Stuart Mill once wrote: "The only way in which a human being can make some approach to knowing the whole of a subject is by hearing what can be said about it by persons of every variety of opinion and studying all modes in which it can be looked at by every character of mind. No wise man ever acquired his wisdom in any mode but this." It is to this principle that Introducing Issues with Opposing Viewpoints books are dedicated.

Introduction

"Life is pleasant. Death is peaceful. It's the transition that's troublesome."

—Isaac Asimov, twentieth-century science-fiction writer

S hunned, marginalized, abused, pitied, and often lied to. This is how Elisabeth Kübler-Ross says dying people were treated in the United States during the 1950s and 1960s, when she was a young psychiatrist. Kübler-Ross treated them differently. She didn't shy away from them and often sat with them for hours listening to them express their feelings. The treatment that dying and terminally ill patients received compelled Kübler-Ross to develop psychiatric techniques that focused on helping them face their impending death. Elisabeth Kübler-Ross's "stages of grief" model has helped innumerable people deal with terminal illness, death, and grief.

Elisabeth Kübler-Ross was born in Switzerland in 1926. After graduating from medical school, she married New Yorker Emanuel Robert Ross in 1958. The couple moved to New York and Kübler-Ross did her residency in psychiatry at various hospitals in the state. At these hospitals, Kübler-Ross noticed that doctors and nurses were uncomfortable with terminally ill people, and dying patients were often isolated and alone. In 1962 Kübler-Ross and her family moved to Colorado, and Kübler-Ross became a teaching fellow at the Colorado School of Medicine in Denver. When she was asked to give a lecture to a class of medical students, she had them interview a sixteen-year-old girl dying of leukemia. At first the medical students asked about blood tests and chemotherapy. But Kübler-Ross urged them to ask the girl how she "felt." The dying girl told them how it made her feel to know that she would never go to her high school prom or go on a date, and she expressed anger at her doctors and nurses for not telling her the truth about her condition. The students then realized that death was more than a clinical condition. A few years later, in 1965, Kübler-Ross, now at the University of Chicago medical school, helped a group of theology students study death. She interviewed dying patients while her students observed behind a two-way mirror. After the theology students' study was completed, Kübler-Ross continued to interview dying people to find out how they felt as they faced their impending death.

By listening to dying people express their feelings, Kübler-Ross began to develop a model for how people come to terms with death. According to the Kübler-Ross model there are five stages dying people go through when they are told they have a terminal illness. These stages are denial, anger, bargaining, depression, and, finally, acceptance. When people reach the stage of acceptance, they have realized that death is inevitable and they can stop fighting and begin to try to gain as much as they can out of the life they have left. Kübler-Ross presented her model in a book titled *On Death and Dying,* which was published in 1969. The book became a best seller and rocked the medical profession. "Dr. Elisabeth Kübler-Ross was a true pioneer in raising the awareness among the physician community and the general public about the important issues surrounding death, dying and bereavement," Dr. Percy Wooten said in 1998, when he was president of the American Medical Association.

The basic components of Kübler-Ross's grief model are still used, although not all workers in the field agree with the model. In *On Death and Dying,* Kübler-Ross said dying people experience the stages of death in order, starting with denial and ending with acceptance. Since then, however, other analysts have noted that the stages of grief can occur in any order and much more rapidly than Kübler-Ross thought. Commenting on the Kübler-Ross model in 2004, psychiatrist Collin Murray Parkes told the *British Medical Journal,* "Like all pioneers, we learn that the new concept is not as simple as initially described. It's no longer considered a linear progression, a one size fits all approach. There's so much more we know today." Another psychoanalyst, John Bowlby, has proposed a grief model that contrasts with the Kübler-Ross model by having only four stages, or phases, of grief. Bowlby's four stages are: (1) shock and numbness (2) yearning and searching (3) disorganization and disorientation, and (4) resolution and reorganization. Some psychiatrists agree with the Bowlby model, but others consider Kübler-Ross's model more effective. Though other researchers have challenged or modified Kübler-Ross's stages of grief model, her book *On Death and Dying* brought public awareness to end-of-life issues and helped both those facing death and their loved ones.

Elisabeth Kübler-Ross dedicated her life to helping dying people. Kübler-Ross wrote more than a dozen books about death and grief. She was a driving force in bringing the hospice movement to America, and she fought for the rights of the dying. She also brought credibility to the field of thanatology, which is the study of death. At her death in August 2004, her close friend Mwalimu Imara said, "Every moment of her life was devoted to dying patients and what they were going through." When Kübler-Ross introduced her stages of grief model in 1969, death was an uncomfortable and even taboo subject in the United States. Some forty years later, the issues of death and dying are a part of mainstream American dialogue. In *Introducing Issues with Opposing Viewpoints: Death and Dying,* the contributors offer their insights and opinions on death and dying in the following chapters: "What Are Americans' Attitudes About Death and Grief?" "How Should the Medical Profession Treat Death?" and "What Happens After Death?"

Chapter 1

What Are Americans' Attitudes About Death and Grief?

Placing flowers on graves is one way people remember those who have died.

Viewpoint

1

Religion Can Ease Grief over Death

"It is hard to devise a [funeral] service which has any meaning which does not fit into a religious ritual."

Julia Neuberger

In the following viewpoint Julia Neuberger contends that funerals, conducted by a priest, pastor, rabbi, imam, or other religious leader, provide a symbolic rite of separation that helps people accept the death of a loved one. According to Neuberger, funerals also offer a place where the community can come together and offer its support and condolences to the bereaved. Even people who are not religious want religious funerals, says Neuberger.

Julia Neuberger is an ordained rabbi, a baroness, and a member of Britain's House of Lords.

AS YOU READ, CONSIDER THE FOLLOWING QUESTIONS:

1. At a funeral, says Neuberger, the resources of the community of faith and the support of friends help the bereaved person to make a choice between what two options?
2. Neuberger refers to rites of separation, rites of transition, and rites of reincorporation. Provide one example for each of these rites.
3. According to Neuberger, in parts of society where religious rituals are not held to be significant there is a noticeable increase in what?

Death has a theological significance in most, if not all, the world's religions. Death is usually the enemy. Death—with its sting—has won. . . . And belief in an afterlife is diminishing in many groups in society. So where those who are providing pastoral care really do believe in God's grace, and/or in eternal life, they are able to bring a kind of certainty of hope that many people find very comforting—even if they, as the recipients of this care, do not wholly believe what is being said themselves. . . .

Of course, those providing pastoral care from the standpoint of a particular religious faith also bring a certain amount of ritual with them in most cases, which many dying people, whatever they actually believe, find very comforting. Social groups, whether secular or religious, tend to develop various rituals to help individuals cope with life crises and transitions. Rituals help people to come to terms with the changes that are happening in their lives. By staging the grieving process, they help people to move from one phase to another.

Funerals Help the Bereaved

Funerals can provide some of this for bereaved people, and the priest, clergyman, rabbi or imam's role at the funeral involves three different aspects. The community of faith, which the priest or whoever represents, can act as a support and help to bereaved people, and indeed often does. For religious people, having death rituals set in the context of some kind of theological understanding helps give an interpretation to the death and the loss. For instance, Christianity can often help bereaved people who are Christians face the loss of death by turning the pain of bereavement into a sense of hope and confidence. The resources of the community of faith, and the support of friends, help the bereaved person make the choice between whether the death of a loved one will remain an open wound, or whether they will move towards building a new life. Going from being wife to widow can be helped by the physical and social event of the funeral, marking for her and for her friends and colleagues and fellow congregants the ending of one phase of her life and the beginning of another.

For Jews and Muslims, to name but two minorities, the support of a community which has particular ways of doing things can also be very comforting, and can help the bereaved come to terms with loss, as they do what they have to do, according to the expectations of their own particular faith group. Indeed, because in those two cases, as with other minorities, the community tends to come out and give support to bereaved people at the time of a death, the dying person and the family or friends often feel the religious community is bringing at least the hope of a kind of a future, without the dying person there, to everyone gathered round. The clergy, as the people who encourage the community to gather round and lend its support, and officiate at the rituals, whatever they might be, bring enormous support to the families.

The real problems come when someone has no religious belief (increasingly common) or belongs to a particular minority commu- nity and has done nothing about it for years, and therefore has no idea what the rituals ought to be, and has a family who are going to be bereaved who have no idea either what the rituals might be. Clergy can be very impatient with people like this, but have a lot to give in

Funerals conducted by religious leaders can provide comfort to family and friends mourning the loss of a loved one.

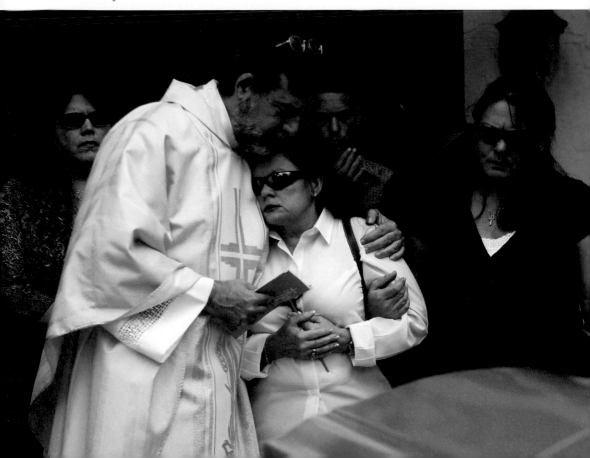

support to those who do not know what to do. More effort from religious communities and their leaders to help those who do not know the rituals to learn them, and, even more importantly, to feel comfortable with them, is urgently needed, and it is a role which the clergy could easily take on board. And it would certainly make dying, and the death rituals, easier for a great many people if that were to happen. . . .

Funeral Is a Rite of Separation

There are several kinds of ritual. There are rites of separation, such as the bar mitzvah of a Jewish boy, or a coming of age ceremony. There are rites of transition, such as a wedding and honeymoon; rites of reincorporation or reunion, such as the dedication of a new home. A funeral service, together with the preparation beforehand which may include preparing the body for burial, and often the family gathering afterwards, has aspects of all three. There is the separation between the grieving family and the one who has died, seen in the lowering of the coffin into the grave, or symbolised by the drawing of a curtain at the crematorium. This helps the bereaved to face the reality of death, particularly where, as in a Jewish burial, the bitter memory is formed of a loud clang of a shovel full of earth landing on the coffin lid. For, unlike common Anglican practice, with a few crumbs of earth being scattered into the hole, Jews and Muslims literally bury their dead, communally. Spadefuls of earth are piled on top of the coffin. The chief mourner puts in the first spadeful, and the other mourners follow suit. There is no doubt that separation is very fully marked by what is a brutal, but useful, tradition. There is no hiding the finality as you hear the lumps of clay descend.

Funerals Are Necessary to Resolve Grief

But the funeral also serves to remind the living to face their own eventual death. The prayers commend the loved one to God's merciful keeping, so that some of the pain of separation is handed to God. But then the mourners commit themselves to God's loving care and protection, whilst the whole congregation becomes a kind of support network. So the funeral, if properly planned and really used for its purpose, can be an important part of the grieving process. It provides a formal and ritual context in which the strong emotions of grief can be appropriately and publicly acknowledged, and in which symbolically the bereaved can be helped by the whole community.

That is vital. Other rituals act as reinforcers of the grieving process, such as the visiting of the 'place of memory', even though no-one, or very few people, believe that the deceased is actually there in any real sense. Partly in the crucially important lonely weeks immediately after the funeral, and partly, also, at significant times like the first anniversary, visiting the grave helps to focus on the passage of time, and, if done in the company of someone else, allows the expression of pastoral support when tears are particularly near the surface, and where, somehow, it is acceptable that they should be.

It is interesting to note that the lack of rituals in mourning may even contribute to an inadequate resolution of grief. In those parts of our society where religious rituals are not held to be significant (which is a growing number as church attendance declines and religious observance generally is on the wane), there is a noticeable increase in the number of counselling agencies offering help to the bereaved. This is because the kind of pastoral care that bereaved people need is not religion specific, though the different theologies make it hard for the clergy of one faith, sometimes, to provide adequate bereavement counselling to people of another. Most pastoral care is, however, practical, though it may be an expression of something more theological. . . .

FAST FACT

According to the American Board of Funeral Service Education, approximately 51 percent of funeral service graduates in 2003 were women, and most graduates were twenty-five to thirty years old.

Religion Informs the Death Process

How we die and how we are buried or cremated, how we grieve and whom we include in our grief, is coloured by different attitudes to death and dying in different cultures. People are variously affected by the religions and cultures in which they grew up, whether or not they have actually practised that particular religion or followed that way of life in the rest of their lives. Catholics who could only be described as 'lapsed'

United States Death Statistics: 1960–2080

Year	U.S. Population	Number of U.S. Deaths	Death Rate per 1,000 Population
1960	179,323,000	1,711,982	9.55
1970	203,302,000	1,921,031	9.45
1980	229,637,000	1,989,841	8.78
1990	248,709,873	2,162,000	8.6
2000	275,306,000	2,403,000	8.7
2010 P*	285,981,000	2,638,000	8.9
2020 P	322,742,000	3,015,000	9.3
2030 P	351,070,000	3,472,000	9.9
2040 P	377,349,000	4,100,000	10.9
2050 P	403,687,000	4,550,000	11.2
2060 P	432,010,000	5,695,000	13.17
2070 P	463,639,000	6,035,000	13.01
2080 P	497,830,000	6,500,000	13.05

*(P) Projected Data

Taken from: National Center for Health Statistics and the Population Division, U.S. Bureau of the Census.

have a tendency to want last rites. Jews who have not been near a synagogue for 50 years want a Jewish burial and someone to say 'kaddish', the mourner's prayer, for them. Sikhs want the ritual readings of the Guru Granth Sahib [the Sikh holy book] even though they have not been near a gurdwara [Sikh temple] for years, and so on. . . .

In many parts of the world, one is defined by how one buries one's dead and mourns them—as a Muslim, a Hindu, a Buddhist, a Zoroastrian, a Sikh. Often, the desire to die in a particular way or to be buried and mourned in a particular way is more about making one's peace with the cultural and religious group from which one comes. It is also, sometimes, to do with a reawakened faith, as a result of thinking time as one approaches one's end. But the motivation is extremely complicated, and often not really capable of being subjected to close analysis.

Religious funerals are also common because people . . . associate ritual mourning with a religious service. . . . So, even for those who never attend church, it is still thought appropriate for a priest or other religious leader to conduct proceedings at the cemetery or the crematorium. That may be partly because, as mentioned above, it is hard to devise a service which has any meaning which does not fit into a religious ritual. . . .

Religious Funerals Are the Norm

Religious funerals of one kind or another are still the norm, and there may be more to it than custom. Clergy of all religions can often help the family in grieving, as can healthcare workers who have been close to the person who has died. In faiths other than Christianity, this might mean helping prepare the body for the funeral, assuring the dying person that he or she will be given a funeral, and preparing for the burial or cremation, in accordance with the customs and rules of the particular religious grouping. In Christianity, it is more likely to be done by the clergy in conjunction with the undertaker, and staff are more used to following the custom of that particular area and Christian belief. At the funeral service itself, the religious leader, of whatever faith, usually acts as leader of the congregation and sets the tone, both of grief and of thanksgiving for the life of the person who has died, in conjunction with the rest of the community where that is appropriate.

EVALUATING THE AUTHOR'S ARGUMENTS:

The author of this viewpoint is an ordained rabbi. What impact, if any, do you think this has on her argument? In your opinion does it strengthen her argument, weaken it, or have no impact? Explain.

Religion Corrupts Death and Does Not Help Grief

"In America . . . threatening religio-theistic perceptions of death, and the fears that they engender, have become integral to the development of a high-income death industry."

Chris Morton

In the following viewpoint Chris Morton proclaims that death and dying in America are difficult for people who do not believe in God or an afterlife. As soon as a person dies, his or her body is kidnapped by an unscrupulous death industry and is inflicted with all kinds of religious rituals, each of which costs an unreasonable amount of money. The vulnerabilities of grieving relatives are exploited throughout the process, asserts Morton. Chris Morton is the New York State director of American Atheists, Inc.

AS YOU READ, CONSIDER THE FOLLOWING QUESTIONS:

1. According to Morton, who said, "Most human beings are taught to face death, like life, as victims—helpless, fearful, resigned?"
2. According to Morton, the body disposal industry is composed of a small yet highly organized group of large companies and a number of smaller companies. How many smaller companies exist?

Chris Morton, "Dying an Atheist in America," *American Atheists, Inc.,* 2006. Reproduced by permission.

3. Morton says some of the "other costs," in addition to body disposal, that will be incurred when he dies, include keeping his corpse in a mortician's freezer and giving mourners a place to congregate and show the family respect. Name three other items that Morton says add to the price of a religious death ceremony.

Dying in America is a complex and distasteful process for most American families and often a taboo subject. As Timothy Leary puts it: "Most human beings are taught to face death, like life, as victims—helpless, fearful, resigned. We're schooled and counseled—programmed to act out a life of scripts based on our worst tendencies toward fear and self-doubt. . . . Throughout history 'fear of dying' has been used by priests, police, politicians, and physicians to undermine individualistic thinking, to increase our dependence on authority and to glorify victimization."

Religious Leaders Want Death to Be Feared

He goes on: "Think of all the hot-button issues that get the church fathers' panties all in a bunch: conception, test-tube fertilization, contraception, out-of-wedlock pregnancy, abortion, euthanasia, suicide, cloning, life extension, out-of-body experiences, occult experimentation, astral travel scenarios, altered states, death-and-rebirth reports, extraterrestrial speculation, cryonics, cyborgization (i.e., replaceable body parts), sperm banks, egg banks, DNA banks, artificial intelligence, artificial life, and personal speculation about experimentation with immortality. All things that experiment with the basic issues of birth, embodiment, and death are anathema to the orthodox seed shepherds, the engineers of the feudal and industrial ages. . . . Why? Because if the flock doesn't fear death, then the grip of religious and political management is broken." The psychological fraternity often considers people who think about death to be ill; terms such as clinically depressed follow them. Death as a cultural/social *bête noire* (something to be avoided) has developed because of the attitudes of formal religions to the end of life, their falsehoods about life after death, or an existence after death (reincarnation, for example), as controlled by a judgmental deity. In America all of these threatening religio-theistic perceptions of death, and the fears that they engender, have become integral to the development of a high-income death industry; pre-death medical treatment, cadaver dressing including makeup, artificial under skin inserts, wigs, freezing, embalming, burials, cremations, urn-production, casket-building, funerals, home visiting, soul saving and church/temple services are all part of this. The Atheist is left in limbo.

As an American Atheist I believe that I am entitled to control my death as I am entitled to control my life—that is part of my right to individual freedom. But the religions do not agree that we have the right to control our deaths, and neither do our political regulating institutions whose members are usually more-or-less Christian. . . .

Religion Forces Expensive and Unscrupulous Rituals on People

After death the Atheist's fight . . . involves the body disposal industry. For the most part, this is a highly organized, small group of large companies, . . . and eight smaller ones, none of whom advertise their services openly, but work under the guise of locally named funeral homes with locally known people—even old families running them. Their aim is not compassion and support for the bereaved, but the collection of the highest fees possible from anguished and emotionally vulnerable relatives. It also involves those who believe that the dying and the dead must be saved from damnation—a highly organized and effective combination when their goals are reinforced by family grief and guilt.

The body disposal industry is, historically, an outgrowth of the religions which still maintain strong influences over it, and often have direct financial ties to it (handouts, direct fees, fee sharing are some of their fiscal arrangements). . . .

Death and body disposal in America are synonymous with past religious practices; the old church-yard with its bent and broken tomb stones, or the memorial chapel, or the ash urns sealed in small cavities behind temple walls, or the cemetery with its crosses and angels and tombs. And the rituals—there are always those rituals. All of these link our current disposal efforts to past religious practices where they prepare the holy receptacle of a departed soul while prayers are said to speed that soul on its way to the good afterlife. Not good places for Atheists to be!

Today a cold and calculating death industry, and often unscrupulous religious groups, try to cater to everyone. The cold, impersonal Unitarian rooms of their "chapels" can be changed at the blink of an eye from an over decorated Roman Catholic wake with open coffin, plastic statues of Mary and Jesus, overflowing flowers, massive crosses and priests and cardinals in scarlet and black

Itemized Services for a Traditional Funeral

June 2007

Services	Average Cost
• Basic Services of Director and Staff	$1,608
• Embalming	$578
• Dressing and Casketing	$196
• Facilities and Staff for Visitation	$367
• Facilities and Staff for Services	$440
• Transfer Vehicle to Funeral Home	$243
• Hearse	$253
• Utility/Flower Vehicle	$137
• Lead Car	$122

Taken from: Everest Information Services, "2007 Funeral Industry Price Comparison Report."

and gold and white, to the plain, almost sterile Jewish shiva with no decorations, no coffin, no flowers, mirrors covered with black cloth, and black-coated rabbis. Each ceremony can be as expensive as another, each ceremony is pumped with religiosity. And somewhere in all of this (or perhaps outside it) the dying Atheist must find a place. . . .

Religious Death Rituals Are Not Cheap

And the other costs? These include keeping my corpse in the mortician's freezer; giving mourners a place to congregate and show the family respect; the flowers; the snacks; the music . . . ; the cars for the entourage; the organization of the burial plot, or the slot in the wall of heavenly peace after the crematorium has sent over someone's ashes—they burn corpses in bunches, so you get a mixture—nice for roses, but not quite what people think they're getting; and the rituals with priests or rabbis or shamans, or whatever.

Everything is modeled on a pseudo-religious ceremony, everything is part of a vision that comes out of a supposed relationship with a deity of some sort. And everything usually costs $10,000.00 and up. Dying isn't cheap. . . .

Atheist Wishes Will Be Ignored

The following things will happen, particularly if Atheists die where nobody knows them, away from their home region. The local body disposal (funeral home) people will whip the body away from the hospital morgue to their refrigerators (remember the costs begin when they leave their funeral parlor) before anyone can do anything and then, because possession is nine-tenths of the law, they will begin their carefully rehearsed process of undermining any alternatives but their own. They will call distraught relatives and say that they have the loved one's body for safekeeping. The relatives will agree, and in their grief they will forget to tell the mortician not to embalm the body. The body will be embalmed. The costs are now around $4,000.00 and rising. If the Atheist's body has been bequeathed to a medical school, they will no longer accept it because it has been tampered with. So the Atheist's body must now be buried or burned.

Embalming tables and equipment at a mortuary give clues to the treatment the body receives by the funeral industry.

I don't fear death at all. As a committed Atheist I have come to terms with the end of my life as a natural, anticipated process. I think about it and talk about it as an everyday item. Dying and death have always seemed to be something final, simple, and very commonplace. But what I do fear, desperately, is the way my fellow non-Atheist humans are going to abuse me as I approach death and after I die. Even though death is final, I feel so sad that my wishes as an Atheist will probably not be taken into consideration. At the end of my life, my non-beliefs will be superseded by others' beliefs because I will no longer have a voice. Because of the insidious involvement of formal religions in every facet of dying and death and instead of continuing to help my species after death as my Atheism demands—I will be thrown away.

EVALUATING THE AUTHOR'S ARGUMENTS:

How would you describe Chris Morton's perception of the funeral industry in America and the tone of his viewpoint? Is it cynical? Sarcastic? Explain. Can you think of any other jobs or industries in America that are perceived similarly?

Viewpoint 3

Belief in a Favorable Afterlife Can Ease Grief over Death

Margaret Paul

"Losing someone we love or facing our own death is never easy. . . . But it is especially difficult and even tortuous when we believe in no God or in a punishing God."

In the following viewpoint Margaret Paul asserts that death and grief are easier for people who believe in a loving God. Paul illustrates her assertion by comparing the death experiences of three young homosexual men whose families had opposing beliefs in God. According to Paul, the family that believed in a compassionate and loving God found comfort in their beliefs and healed their grief.

Margaret Paul has created a six-step spiritual healing process. She is an author and public speaker.

AS YOU READ, CONSIDER THE FOLLOWING QUESTIONS:
1. What was David's religious background? What was Thomas's?
2. Where does fear come from, according to Paul?
3. According to Paul, how do we know that something is true for us?

Margaret Paul, "Death and Dying: Tragedy or Opportunity?" *Soulful Living Connections,* Spring/Summer, 2007. Reproduced by permission of the author.

Our response to any situation in our lives is a direct result of our beliefs concerning that situation. Our individual and societal beliefs concerning what dying is and what happens after death create many of the feelings that result when we are faced with a life-threatening illness or with losing a loved one. The fact that our experience, feelings and behavior follow directly from our beliefs is illustrated in the following examples describing divergent belief systems concerning death and dying.

David, Thomas and Richard were all young, homosexual men who died of AIDS.

Terrified of Death

David came from a Jewish humanistic/atheistic heritage and had adopted the same beliefs as his parents. His parents loved him dearly and had accepted his sexual orientation as part of their humanistic beliefs. Having no spiritual beliefs or experiences, they have no concept of anything beyond this life. To them, the soul is not separate from the body. Faced with the prospect of their son dying, they were devastated. To them, he would disappear forever into nothingness, a thought they could not bear. David, sharing their beliefs, was terrified of the thought of complete annihilation. Because death to him meant the end of his existence, he spent his last days fighting it, too terrified to give in, even though he was in great pain. When David finally died, his parents became depressed and somewhat bitter. Their son was gone forever. They felt helpless and hopeless and never quite recovered from their loss.

Thomas came from a Fundamentalist Christian background. Both he and his parents considered him to be flawed, less than perfect in the eyes of God. They believed that, because of his sexual orientation, he could not enter the gates of heaven. Thomas's life had been a torture of self-recrimination over who he was, and during his illness both he and his parents believed he was being punished for being who he was. Death was terrifying to Thomas as he imagined himself locked forever in Hell. His parents, angry and bitter over the prospective loss of their son, took some of this out on him, blaming him for being gay. Thomas and his parents faced his death with fear and anger. After his death, his parents were stoic on the outside and deeply grief-stricken on the inside, with no way to heal the grief.

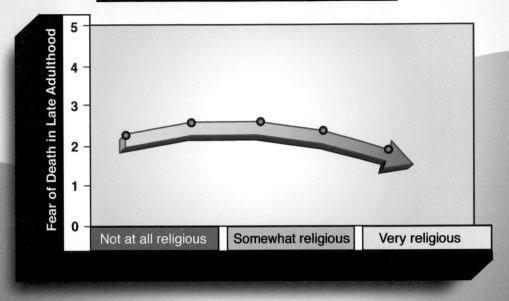

Religiousness and Fear of Death

Fear of Death in Late Adulthood

Not at all religious | Somewhat religious | Very religious

Taken from: "Does Religiousness Buffer Against the Fear of Death and Dying in Late Adulthood?" Paul Wink and Julia Scott, *Journal of Gerontology, Psychological Sciences*, July 2005.

Dying Is Not Punishment or Tragedy

Richard was raised in a liberal Christian family with strong spiritual values, which were greatly influenced by Native American and Eastern philosophies. His family, close-knit and accepting, did not often attend church but brought their loving, compassionate God into their every-day lives. They accepted their son's sexual orientation with equanimity, and he never stopped experiencing their unconditional love. Richard and his family believed that life on planet earth is part of an eternal journey of the soul as it evolves toward oneness with Spirit. They believe that our real home is in the spiritual realm, and that death is no more than a shedding of this temporary house of the soul as the soul returns home once again. They believe they will see each other again in the spirit realm, and that dying is not a punishment or a tragedy but just an indication that the lessons on schoolhouse earth are complete for this time around. They see the dying process as another opportunity for learning and growing in their lovingness, and they see death as a transition into new learning opportunities. They felt deep sorrow and grief at the thought of not being together in the flesh, but knowing they would always be together in spirit left them filled rather than empty. Richard approached his dying process as part of his life experience and was surrounded with love when he left his body. His family expressed their sorrow and grief freely, and also their joy that he was out of pain, that his transition was peaceful and that he is in a more beautiful place. They are sad for themselves because they miss him but they are happy for him that he has moved on to his real home. They hold and comfort each other lovingly each time their grief comes up, allowing healing to occur through their shared love and sorrow. They pray for him daily and connect with him in their dreams. His loss motivated them to help other families who have children dying of AIDS.

Creating a New View of Death and Dying

Losing someone we love or facing our own death is never easy. We all become attached to this earthly level, attached to our bodies as being part of who we are. But it is especially difficult and even tortuous when we believe in no God or in a punishing God.

Creating a new view of death and dying means changing our belief system. The question is, how can we do this? If, like David, we have had no spiritual beliefs, or like Thomas we believe in a punishing God, how can we change this? We cannot change our beliefs only on the level of our minds. Our beliefs change only when we have a new experience and in order to have this new experience we have to be *willing* to have it. If we want to stay with our old beliefs, then, of course, we will be unwilling to open to anything new. The first step, then, in changing our belief system is our willingness to have a new experience. Once we are willing, then we can open our heart to having a new experience by deciding that we are ready to learn about the truth— we are ready to question our cherished beliefs and receive an experience of our truth. Once we are open to learning, we can explore our present belief system and trace it back to its origins, connecting our fears regarding death and dying with our belief system. Fear comes from false beliefs:

False
Evidence
Appearing
Real

Learning to Believe in a Loving God

After we understand the beliefs that create our fears of death and dying, we can then open our hearts to Higher Guidance, imagining a coach, a mentor, a teacher, or an angel—someone we imagine within us or outside of us who is filled with wisdom and love. As we imagine talking with and listening to this wise being, we will tap into our truth. Our truth is always available for us when we truly open to it with a deep desire to learn. Learning our truth may take time. We may hear it in our own imaginations through words, pictures, or feelings. We may hear it through the mouths of others, through reading, through dreams. Our truth comes to us in different ways, but we will recognize it only when we are looking for it.

Grieving may be eaiser for those who believe their loved ones have gone to a better place.

Once we begin to hear our truth and bring it down to our feeling level—the wounded child within who has the false beliefs—we can then take action based upon our new truth. This means living our lives based on this truth. What would you be doing differently if you believed that your soul is not only eternal, but that you are eternally loved by an unconditionally loving God, which means that you are loved no matter what? What if punishment is something you do to yourself through your own false beliefs rather than something imposed upon you from God? What if all of life's difficulties are challenges for you to move more and more into lovingness and the full manifestation of your Self? What if you are on a wonderful, creative, eternal journey to evolve the very fabric of love—of God—through evolving your own lovingness? What if becoming a more loving human being is your sacred purpose and your sacred privilege? How would you be living your life differently if you believed the above?

The way we *know* something is true for us is if it brings us peace and joy rather than fear. Darkness brings fear. Lies bring fear. Truth brings joy and peace. The more we open to truth and act on it, the more peaceful and joyful we feel, about life and about death and dying. Thus, taking action based upon new beliefs will lead to knowing what is true for us.

These six steps: Willingness, Opening to Learning, Exploring Beliefs with Wounded Self, Exploring Truth and Loving Action with Higher Self, Taking Loving Action, and Evaluating the Action can lead us to the healing of our false beliefs concerning who we are, what God is, what our purpose is, and anything else. Healing our false beliefs and living in our truth completely changes our experience of life and our experience of death.

EVALUATING THE AUTHOR'S ARGUMENTS:

Margaret Paul supports her viewpoint using anecdotal evidence, which is supplied by the stories of David, Thomas, and Richard. Anecdotal evidence is based on casual observations rather than statistics or scientific information. Can you think of any statistics that might support this author's argument?

Belief in a Favorable Afterlife Devalues Life

John Bice

"*If an eternal and infinitely preferable life exists subsequent to this one, human life is diminished.*"

In the following viewpoint John Bice contends that the religious belief in an eternal and idyllic afterlife has many harmful consequences. Bice says suicide bombers are motivated to kill thousands of innocent people because they believe they will receive heavenly rewards after their deaths. Additionally, contends Bice, many people endure unnecessary misery in their lives, mistakenly thinking they will be rewarded in heaven.

John Bice is an author and writer employed by Michigan State University.

AS YOU READ, CONSIDER THE FOLLOWING QUESTIONS:

1. When was Albigensianism practiced, according to Bice?
2. According to Bice, what reason does author Sam Harris give for why nineteen well-educated, middle-class men carried out the September 11, 2001, terrorist attacks?
3. Who said that "for the believing Christian, death is no big deal," according to the author?

John Bice, "Afterlife Concept Devalues Earthly Existence; Celebrates Death," *State News,* October 21, 2005. Reproduced with permission.

Unsubstantiated belief, also known as "religious faith," can produce unwelcome consequences. Among the most potentially dangerous is the belief in a heavenly and eternal afterlife, since this notion inherently degrades and devalues our earthly existence.

If no afterlife exists, our lives are finite, unique and precious. There are no second chances or rewards; when we die, we're dead.

Alternatively, if an eternal and infinitely preferable life exists subsequent to this one human life is diminished. An everlasting and flawlessly idyllic afterlife, overflowing with ineffable delights, means that our earthly existence—no matter how long it lasts or relatively good it might be—is insignificant and less desirable in comparison.

Biding Time

More than one Christian, when pressed, has admitted to me that they're essentially "biding their time," avoiding sin and waiting for their eternal reward. How sad.

Perhaps this explains why many religious regard suicide as a grave mortal sin. Without such prohibition, certainty of belief in heaven could prompt highly faithful people to shorten their earthly lives and hasten their trip to paradise, which would translate into fewer congregants.

Viewing the evolution of religion from a Darwinian perspective, . . . one would expect successful modern faiths to discourage suicide and promote sexual reproduction, which is precisely what we see. Suicidal cults, or faiths that discourage procreation, are at a tremendous competitive disadvantage for passing on their beliefs.

> ## FAST FACT
>
> *AARP The Magazine* surveyed 1,011 Americans over the age of fifty and found that 73 percent believe in life after death and that belief in an afterlife has risen in the last fifty years.

Albigensianism, a Christian faith practiced in the Middle Ages, offers an example of an extinct religion that reportedly embraced these maladaptive and self-limiting dogmatic approaches. This cult believed the earthly physical realm was evil, frowned on procreation, and condoned suicide by starvation as a way of freeing spirits from their earth-bound prisons. It's impossible to know how long this cult would have lasted, however, since the Roman Catholic Church hunted down and exterminated these "heretics" during the Albigensian Crusade.

Reward After Death Spurs Suicide Bombers

Regrettably, fervent belief in an afterlife can motivate people well beyond thoughts of personal suicide. Author Sam Harris, discussing the Sept. 11 [2001] terrorist attacks, wrote, "why did 19 well-educated, middle-class men trade their lives for the privilege of killing thousands of our neighbors? Because they believed, on the authority of the Quran, that they would go straight to paradise for doing so."

A fascinating *Time* magazine article, "Inside the Mind of an Iraqi Suicide Bomber," offered a glimpse at the mentality behind such attacks. "The happiest day of my life," was how Iraqi Jihadist Marwan

Suicide bombers are willing to sacrifice their lives, believing they will be rewarded after death.

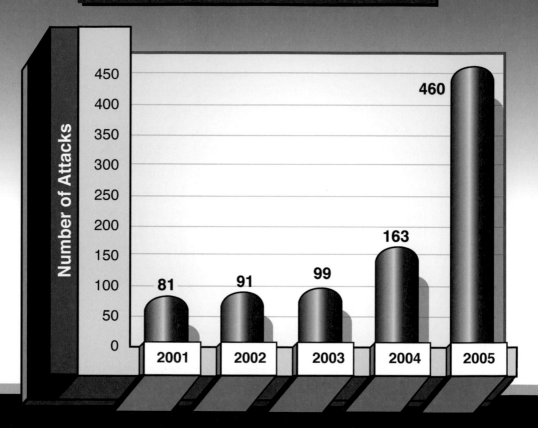

Suicide Attacks Worldwide, 2001–2005

Number of Attacks

Year	Number
2001	81
2002	91
2003	99
2004	163
2005	460

Taken from: Scott Atran, "The Moral Logic and Growth of Suicide Terrorists," *Washington Quarterly*, spring 2006.

Abu Ubeida described feeling after being added to a long list of suicide bomber volunteers. Marwan enthusiastically declared, "I can't wait. . . . I am ready to die now." Only blind religious faith, or insanity, can provide such joyful excitement to kill and die.

Faith in heavenly reward isn't the only conceivable rationale for a suicide attack. Other motivations might include extreme political, nationalistic or ethnic factors combined with feelings of desperation. Nevertheless, an enthusiastic and seemingly endless supply of suicide bombers is unquestionably enhanced by widespread belief in paradise, particularly one stocked with abundant and eager to please young virgin women. Atheists, and others who lack similarly appealing fantasies of faith, make extraordinarily poor candidates for suicide bombers.

More Problems with Afterlife Delusions

It's tempting to dismiss this devaluation of human life as merely a radical Muslim phenomenon; however, that's not the case. I'll let U.S. Supreme Court Justice, and radical Christian conservative, Antonin Scalia make that point.

Scalia, speaking on the subject of the death penalty to the University of Chicago Divinity School, made this frighteningly accurate observation: "The more Christian a country is, the less likely it is to regard the death penalty as immoral. . . . I attribute that to the fact that for the believing Christian, death is no big deal."

Scalia is right. Death is "no big deal" for the truly faithful, and that's a problem. Faith-based afterlife delusions have consequences beyond suicide bombings and nonchalant attitudes toward capital punishment; for an inestimable number of people it has resulted in lifetimes of forbidden pleasures, self-denial and unnecessary misery endured explicitly to achieve the hypothetical "eternal reward."

[Feminist] Gloria Steinem concisely summarizes the problem, "spirituality celebrates life, religion celebrates life after death."

EVALUATING THE AUTHOR'S ARGUMENTS:

Bice quotes an author, a *Time* magazine article, and a Supreme Court justice. What impact do you think quoting from these sources has on Bice's argument? Explain.

Sometimes It Is Best to Accept Death

Tom Nesi

"I think we need to ask ourselves whether offering terminal patients limited hope of a few more months is really beneficial."

In the following viewpoint Tom Nesi describes his wife's death from a deadly form of cancer. The "miracle" drugs she took to fight the cancer extended her life by a few months. However, after watching his wife become depressed and suffer myriad side effects from the drugs, Nesi came to the conclusion that the costs of life-extending measures are sometimes too great to bear. Tom Nesi is a communications and education specialist in the health-care field.

AS YOU READ, CONSIDER THE FOLLOWING QUESTIONS:
1. According to Nesi, what national agency will the Food and Drug Administration be working with to accelerate the development and approval of cancer drugs?
2. With which type of brain cancer was Nesi's wife diagnosed? According to Nesi, what is the average survival time for patients with this disease?
3. According to Nesi, his wife's treatment cost at least how much?

Tom Nesi, "False Hope in a Bottle," *New York Times*, June 5, 2003. Reproduced by permission.

S even months ago, I made the decision to hasten the end of my wife's life. Susan lay in an irreversible coma and had not been fed for 10 days; she was being kept alive solely by fluids. An old family friend stopped by with advice that no one in the medical profession had been able to offer.

"You need to stop giving your wife liquid," he said.

I shook my head. "You cannot deprive a living being of water," I said.

"Your wife is no longer with us," he said. "She died of a brain tumor two weeks ago. Susan needs to rest now."

I still refused to accept the fact and called several of Susan's doctors and members of our family. Each of them reaffirmed that withholding fluid was the humane decision. Indeed, in her living will Susan had spelled out that she did not want "artificial prolongation" of her life either through nutrition or hydration.

New Cancer Drugs for the Desperately Ill

For about a year, Susan had been offered numerous medications, including, in the latter stages of her illness, Iressa, which last month [May 2003] was approved by the Food and Drug Administration (FDA) despite limited data about its effectiveness. Two other experimental drugs, Avastin and Erbitux, are now going through the FDA approval process. With the release . . . of new clinical studies, many believe the chances of approval have greatly improved. The process will likely be helped by the FDA's new program . . . to work with the National Cancer Institute to accelerate the development and approval of cancer drugs.

It is hard to argue against making new cancer drugs available to the desperately ill. Certainly, these drugs are a step in the right direction in the fight against the disease. But so far they have been proved only to

> **FAST FACT**
>
> Only 20 percent of doctors' survival predictions for terminally ill patients are correct. Sixty-three percent of the time, doctors think terminal patients have more time than they do, according to studies reported in the *British Medical Journal* in 2000 and 2003.

extend life by a few months in patients whose cancer has been diagnosed as virtually incurable. I think we need to ask ourselves whether offering terminal patients limited hope of a few more months is really beneficial. The question is not whether days are extended, but in what condition the patient lives and at what emotional and financial cost.

Hoping for More Time

My wife was discovered to have glioblastoma, a deadly form of brain cancer, in August 2001. She was 52. The average survival time for patients with this disease is about 11 months. We, of course, hoped for more time.

Susan was treated at a prestigious medical center with access to a wide array of innovative drugs, including a Gliadel wafer, which delivered chemotherapy directly to the site of her tumor. On average, we were told, this treatment extends life by about two months. But Susan

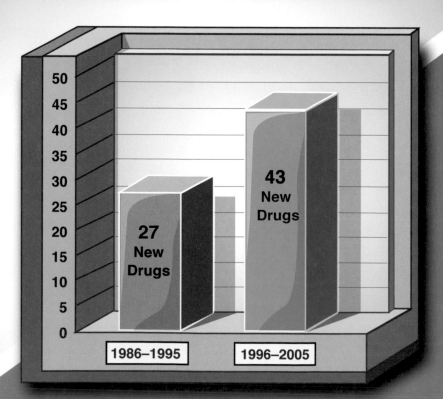

Cancer Drug Approval Rates, 1986–2005

27 New Drugs — 1986–1995

43 New Drugs — 1996–2005

Taken from: U.S. Food and Drug Administration.

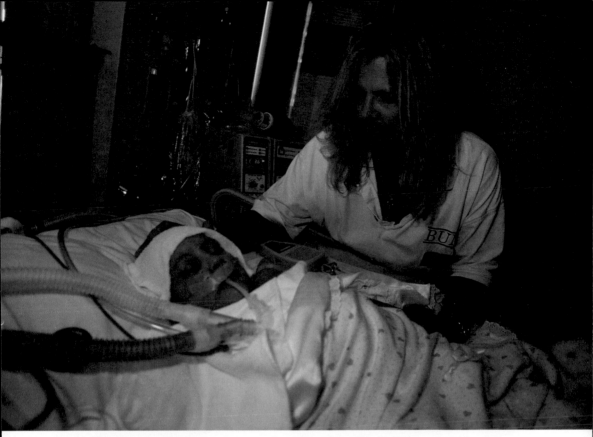

In some cases cancer treatments may only prolong the suffering of the patient.

suffered a great many problems over the next few horrific months. She was hospitalized five more times and had two more brain surgeries. After a third surgery, she had a stroke that left her almost totally paralyzed and unable to speak or eat—leaving me with the decision to take her off life support.

A Terrible Price for Three More Months

But according to the medical profession, the experimental treatment had worked. Susan lived almost three months longer than the average patient with glioblastoma. Somewhere in some computer database, Susan's experimental regimen will be counted a success. She was a "responder." And therein lies the terrible truth behind the approval of "miracle drugs" on the basis of "tumor shrinkage" or "extended days." Susan's life was extended. But at what cost?

During those final months, we incurred expenses for four ambulance trips, two weeks in a critical care center, a full-time home health-care aide, a feeding tube and electronic monitor, home hospital equipment, occupational therapists, social workers and medication. My wife's treatment cost at least $200,000 (most of which, fortunately, was covered by insurance). I had to greatly curtail my work schedule and hire someone to handle the myriad bills.

I still hear the words of my wife's surgeon after her disastrous third surgery: "We have saved your wife's life. . . . We have given you the ability to spend more quality time with your loved one." And the words she scribbled on a notepad two weeks later: "depressed . . . no more . . . please."

Peace at Last

Susan's last half hour was peaceful. We gave her morphine. Her eyes fluttered. I held her hand. Finally, her breathing stopped. On the table next to her were hundreds of pills, nutrition bottles, vials, needles. No longer needed.

EVALUATING THE AUTHOR'S ARGUMENTS:

Do you think Tom Nesi makes a convincing argument? Why or why not? Would your evaluation of his argument change if he described the death of someone he did not really know instead of his wife's death? Is his viewpoint personal? Explain.

Viewpoint
6

It Is Always Best to Fight Death

Andrew W. Saul

"Death is to be denied, fought and beaten for as long as possible."

In the following viewpoint Andrew W. Saul speaks to people suffering from terminal illnesses and tells them to keep fighting and never give up. No one knows how long they have to live, and doctors' prognoses can be wrong, he says. Saul also speaks to doctors and gives them ways to help their terminally ill patients live longer. Andrew W. Saul is an author, a teacher, a consultant in natural healing, and the editor in chief of the *Orthomolecular Medicine News Service.*

AS YOU READ, CONSIDER THE FOLLOWING QUESTIONS:
1. According to Saul, what is an indication that the body is saturated with carotene?
2. Instead of reading the *Journal of the American Medical Association,* what journal does Saul recommend doctors treating terminal patients read?
3. According to Saul, for a terminally ill patient, what is the most important improvement of all?

All terminal patients need to be reminded that while there is life, there is more than hope alone. . . .

A condition may be serious, and generally considered fatal by expert medical opinion. Well, expert opinion has been wrong before this. . . .

You risk nothing when you acknowledge desperation. Health practitioners often hide from patients when they think nothing more can be done. Too bad, because desperate patients work harder. Harness that will to live and go for it. . . .

Fight Disease and Death

Death is to be denied, fought and beaten for as long as possible. There is too much talk about "preparing for death," "putting affairs in order" and "accepting death as a fact of life." You can if you want, but I will never negotiate with death. Death is described as the "last enemy" in

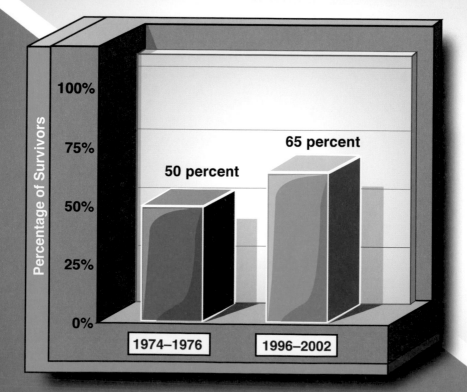

Cancer Survival Rates in the United States

Percentage of Survivors

100%

75% 65 percent

50 percent

50%

25%

0%

1974–1976   1996–2002

Taken from: U.S. Food and Drug Administration.

the Bible. We're all going to go, but we certainly don't have to go quietly. Life may be fatal to everyone, but it doesn't have to be today and it doesn't have to be you. Don't wait until you hear the rattle of death; duck and run for it now. Is this an attitude of "denying" death? Not really. In Africa, we did not deny the existence of lions by avoiding them. Keep fighting, and don't worry about hurting death's feelings by doing it.

Medical doctors generally fight disease with one hand tied behind their backs. This is because they arrogantly assume that if they don't know it, it isn't knowable or worth knowing. Baloney. Aggressive use of vitamins and radical diet revision DO have their place in the science of therapeutics. Besides, if someone is going to die anyway, what have they got to lose?

Take Vitamin C
Body saturation of Vitamin C is indicated by diarrhea. Saturation of carotene is indicated by orange skin. Saturation of niacin is indicated by flushing. In order, these are the benchmarks of maximum use of the most powerful antibiotic-antiviral, cancer/heart disease preventer, and mind-calmer in nature. If you are really sick, and still haven't tried these, then you haven't lived yet. If you are breathing, you haven't died yet.

> ## FAST FACT
>
> In response to demand for experimental drugs, a U.S. appeals court ruled in August 2007 that terminally ill patients do not have a constitutional right to unapproved products.

How Doctors Can Help the Terminally Ill to Live
Practitioners, here are four steps to harnessing the life force even in grave cases.

A. LISTEN to the patient; they will tell you more than technology ever can. Patients will tell you why they are sick, and it is as likely to be from misery as from microbes. Don't forget stress reduction training, counseling, clergy, hugs.

B. KNOW about nutrition and vitamin therapies and ALL possible options. Never say never, and do your homework. Were he a physician,

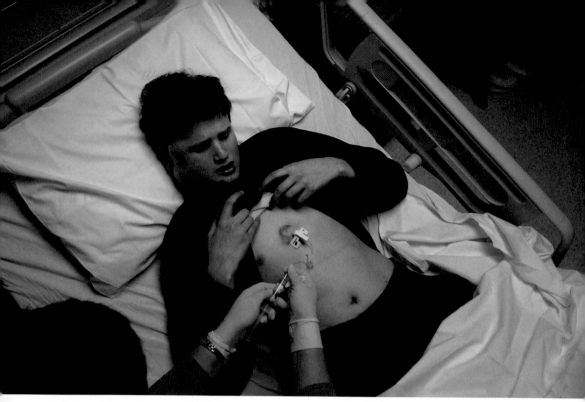

A teenager undergoes experimental gene therepy where antibodies are infused through a port implanted in the boy's chest.

[humorist] Will Rogers might have said "All I know is what I read in the journals." Get your nose out of *JAMA* [the *Journal of the American Medical Association*] and read other journals, such as *American Journal of Clinical Nutrition* and *Journal of Orthomolecular Medicine*. Doctor, if you are too busy to seriously investigate alternatives, then you are too busy. . . .

C. Access your patient and COMMUNICATE knowledge, one adult to another. Provide your references and give homework. As you did yours, the patient should do theirs. It only takes half a minute to provide a patient with an alternative medicine reading list and the suggestion, "Take vitamins, become a vegetarian, get and use a juicer, and load up on Vitamin C." I'm NOT saying that this is a sure cure but rather that it is a very potent and very low risk additional measure.

D. MOTIVATE and stimulate the patient to want to try all possible healing approaches. We do not trivialize medicine nor do we guarantee miracles when we urge alternatives. Doctors and patients alike must do everything possible to get well. Every physician is duty bound to offer ALL options "for the good of the patient, to the best of my ability" [as per the Hippocratic oath]. Your ability includes offering encouragement. Build a fire and fan it.

Always Be Optimistic

For a terminal patient, any improvement at all is cause for celebration. Slowing the rate of decline is improvement. Stabilization is better. Some recovery is better still. Cure is, of course, the best. Improved length of life is a major goal, but improved quality of life is the most important of all.

The only thing good about yesterday's obituary column is that you weren't in it, and the proof is that you are reading this today. The people that didn't make it have no bearing on you. Will Rogers was once told that parachutes in airplanes would probably only save one person per crash. He answered, "But wouldn't he be just tickled!"

I have worked with the dying, and have come into intensive care units to find beds empty that yesterday contained a friend. Sometimes it was because he'd died during the night. Sometimes it was because she went home well. No one, but no one, knows how long they have to live, whether sick or not.

EVALUATING THE AUTHORS' ARGUMENTS:

The author of the previous viewpoint believes that terminally ill cancer patients should not always fight death by taking new cancer drugs. Do you think Saul recommends taking new cancer drugs to fight death? If not, what does he seem to recommend? Explain.

Chapter 2

How Should the Medical Profession Treat Death?

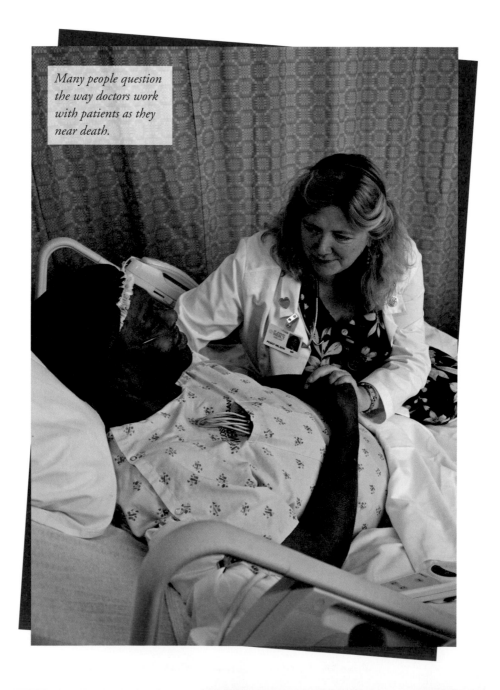

Many people question the way doctors work with patients as they near death.

Doctors Should Assist with Death

Tom Preston

> *"Is it God's will that we may not end a life after we have artificially extended it to a state of ungodly suffering?"*

In the following viewpoint Tom Preston maintains that physician-assisted suicide (PAS) is ethical and merciful. Preston says that arguments against PAS that are based on the sanctity of life are flawed. He says that modern medicine routinely distorts the naturalness of death, and hence the sanctity of life, when the lives and the suffering of the dying are prolonged by artificial means. When dying people want to hasten their death, it isn't suicide says Preston, and when doctors help them, it isn't killing. Tom Preston, a physician and author, is on the board of directors of Compassion and Choices of Washington.

AS YOU READ, CONSIDER THE FOLLOWING QUESTIONS:
1. What are some legal and ethical methods that Preston says doctors already use to stop pain and suffering and help patients die?
2. According to Preston, when and how did the sanctity of life principle evolve?
3. In a medically managed process of dying, what three options for ending a patient's life does Preston say are equally ethical?

The Oregon Death with Dignity Act has worked nearly perfectly for more than eight years, giving peaceful dying to 246 patients and backup security to thousands more, with no evidence of misuse of the law. Sad to say, unfounded fears and old taboos have kept Washington from doing as well for its residents.

Dying Is No Longer Natural

This backwardness is largely because Americans don't understand how dying has changed, and their obsolete notions of acceptable ways of dying cause a lot of end-of-life suffering. Dying is not an isolated event but a process beginning with a fatal illness. In the past, dying was swifter, as with pneumonia, but our advanced medical interventions now extend dying for weeks, months or years. We no longer die "naturally" but live longer with chemotherapy, surgery, artificial pacemakers, organ transplants and more.

Modern medicine gives us extra years of good life, but when interventions such as chemotherapy or bypass surgery prolong life they also change how we ultimately die. People—medical workers with

In Oregon, where assisted suicide is legal, doctors can provide terminally ill patients with prescriptions for lethal doses of phenobarbital.

their technologies—fashion our new ways of dying, and too often patients linger with suffering before the end. Most Americans die in medical facilities, sustained for the last weeks of life with drugs, feeding tubes and artificial ventilators.

It's Someone's Decision—Why Not the Patient's?

Doctors already directly help patients die, in order to stop pain and suffering, with legal and ethical methods such as morphine drips or continuous drug-induced unconsciousness, or by withdrawing artificial ventilators or other means of life support. The majority of patients today die after a human decision—made by doctor, family member or other—to stop further treatment that would only prolong suffering. The process of dying for most of us is a series of medical decisions culminating when someone decides how we will die.

The issue for most of us will be, "Who decides how and when will we die?" We have pre-empted natural dying with our medical interventions, so why shouldn't the patient decide the mode and time of dying, consistent with his or her values, rather than leaving it to the ravages of "doing everything possible" or the whim of the medical resident on call?

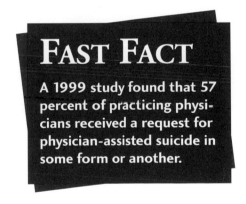

FAST FACT

A 1999 study found that 57 percent of practicing physicians received a request for physician-assisted suicide in some form or another.

Distorting the Sanctity of Life

Many would say, "It is a violation of God's will, or the sanctity of life, to help someone die sooner than is natural." The sanctity of life principle evolved in the Middle Ages, when St. Thomas Aquinas equated God's will with what is natural. But the unending work of modern medicine is to prevent natural dying and to give us longer than natural lives. When a doctor maintains life with an artificial ventilator, he has created unnatural life, and when he turns off the breathing machine months later, life ends unnaturally.

We distort the meaning of the sanctity of life by saying we must sanctify all life, however artificial and harmful it has become. Is it

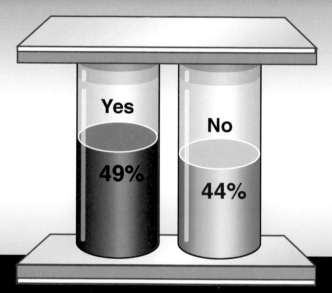

Americans Polled May 10–13, 2007

Yes
No
49%
44%

Taken from: Gallup Poll News Service.

God's will that we may not end a life after we have artificially extended it to a state of ungodly suffering?

In the totality of a medically managed process of dying, the last individual human act—deciding how a patient will die—is equally ethical whether sedating the patient until death, stopping life-support therapy such as kidney dialysis or giving a patient the means of voluntarily ending life with lethal pills.

It's Not Suicide or Killing

A patient who self-administers lethal pills is not committing suicide. Suicide is of a person who does not have to die, and who has a treatable or manageable disorder. On the other hand, a terminally ill person (the law in Oregon requires terminal illness for aid in dying) has no means of cure or long-term management of his illness, is irreversibly dying and does not commit suicide by choosing one means of medical dying over another.

Further, a physician who prescribes lethal pills a dying patient may or may not use is not assisting suicide any more than when he stops life support or sedates a patient to the time of death. Nor is he "killing," a phrase used by opponents to generate fear of assisted dying. To kill is "to deprive of life," and a dying patient who self-administers pills achieves his goal—he is not deprived or killed.

Once we have prolonged life as much as is reasonable without causing undue suffering, we have honored our obligation—and that of the state—to protect and sanctify life. Assisting dying for terminally ill patients is then ethical and merciful, and—as in Oregon—is safe. If ours is a humane and caring society we should make it legal.

EVALUATING THE AUTHORS' ARGUMENTS:

Does the fact that Tom Preston is a physician give greater weight to his argument? Why or why not? The author of the following viewpoint is also a physician. Which physician do you think makes a stronger case for his views? Explain.

Doctors Should Not Assist with Death

David C. Stolinksy

> *"About 2400 years ago, Hippocrates told physicians to heal and never to kill."*

In the following viewpoint David C. Stolinsky contends that physician-assisted suicide (PAS) is morally and ethically wrong and doctors who participate in it are violating the Hippocratic oath. Stolinsky says that U.S. courts and lawyers, such as those who sanctioned Oregon's law—to date the only state allowing PAS—are not asking the right question. It isn't a legal question, says Stolinsky, it's a moral question. He believes that the medical profession needs "an infusion of moral principles and ethical values." David C. Stolinsky is a conservative political commentator and a medical doctor.

AS YOU READ, CONSIDER THE FOLLOWING QUESTIONS:

1. According to Stolinsky, the *New England Journal of Medicine* articles only contained references to court decisions and legal sources, but not one reference to what?
2. According to the author, once the Nazis took over, medical graduates no longer took the Hippocratic oath. Instead, they took an oath to what?
3. When you check out the court cases that authorized assisted suicide or euthanasia, what names will you find, according to Stolinsky?

I regret to say that I just received the latest issue of the *New England Journal of Medicine,* one of the most influential medical journals. Besides the scientific articles, there were two additional articles. Both articles dealt with assisted suicide. Both articles were written from a legal, not a moral, point of view.

The articles dealt with the [2006] U.S. Supreme Court decision that upheld Oregon's assisted suicide law, and forbade the Justice Department to interfere with it. The Oregon law allows doctors to prescribe lethal doses of controlled substances like morphine to patients who request it and are "terminally" ill—that is, expected to die in six months.

It Is a Moral Question

To me, the question is whether killing a patient is ethical. To the *New England Journal,* the question is whether killing a patient is permitted under the federal Controlled Substances Act.

How are these questions to be answered? An ethical question must be answered by reference to ethical standards such as the Hippocratic Oath. This oath has been taken by young physicians for 2400 years. It states:

> *I will give no deadly medicine to anyone if asked, nor suggest any such counsel.*

The two articles I refer to totaled 5539 words. But the words "Hippocratic" or "Oath" are not among them. Nor is there any mention of the position of Catholic, Protestant, Jewish or Muslim theologians on assisted suicide or euthanasia. So much for "multicultural-ism," which never was about different cultures, but only about shredding our own culture.

The articles had many references to court decisions and legal sources, but not one reference to any source of ethical wisdom. For the authors and the editors, there was no need to include anything except legal references. For these people, there were no moral questions, only legal ones. And, of course, legal questions are answered by judges. . . .

Killing as "Healing" Started in Nazi Germany

Since ancient times, society assigned the task of saving life to physicians. If killing people was required, that task was given to executioners. Now we have confused these opposite roles.

Many people believe that doctor-assisted suicide is morally wrong.

A milestone on the road downhill was the publication in Germany in 1920 of "Permission to Exterminate Life Unworthy of Life." The "unworthy" included the incurably ill, the mentally ill or retarded, deformed children and the comatose. Killing was "healing treatment" to be administered by physicians.

For the first time, killing and healing were mixed together. And physicians' loyalty was no longer to the individual patient, but to "society" or the state.

Once the Nazis took over, medical graduates no longer took the Hippocratic Oath, but an oath to the health of the state. Most American medical graduates also no longer take the Hippocratic Oath, but a variety of other oaths, of which only 8 percent reject abortion, and only 14 percent reject euthanasia. This is called "progress."

I believe the chief cause of the Hippocratic Oath's demise is its ban on abortion. But in the Oath, euthanasia and abortion are next to each other. Discarding one prohibition weakened the other. If *all* human life isn't sacred, none is. Intermediate positions are weak and are being overrun one by one. Who is worthy to live becomes just a matter of opinion.

The phrase "life unworthy of life" was used by the Nazis, but it originated before anyone heard of Hitler. Nazism was a seed that fell on soil that had already been fertilized by the manure of viewing human beings not as having intrinsic worth because they are created in God's image, but as having worth *only if they are useful to others.*

Those who now spread similar manure will not be able to claim innocence if similar seeds sprout. The lesson of history is clear.

The Nazi euthanasia program used drugs, then gas, and was the physical and psychological prelude to the Holocaust. It was opposed so strongly by Catholic and

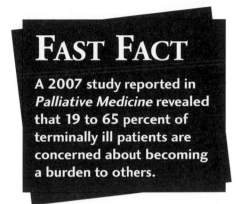

FAST FACT

A 2007 study reported in *Palliative Medicine* revealed that 19 to 65 percent of terminally ill patients are concerned about becoming a burden to others.

Protestant churches that it was stopped, though it continued unofficially. Sadly, there was no organized opposition by physicians.

Of all professions, medicine had the highest percent of Nazis. When leading doctors support late-term abortion, assisted suicide, euthanasia, and cloning of human embryos, remember not to expect moral leadership from the medical profession. This lesson is also clear. . . .

Once we throw away the rulebook, the referee becomes a dictator.

Check out the court cases that authorized assisted suicide or euthanasia. You'll find the names Nancy Cruzan, Karen Ann Quinlan and Elizabeth Bouvia. They were women, as were Terri Schiavo and most of the people killed by Dr. Kevorkian. Being disabled is becoming dangerous, but being a disabled woman is more dangerous. That doesn't trouble most ethicists or judges. Of course, the majority of them are men. . . .

The Medical Profession Is Killing Itself

As I write these words, I look up at the wall and see the copy of the Hippocratic Oath I was given when I graduated from medical school

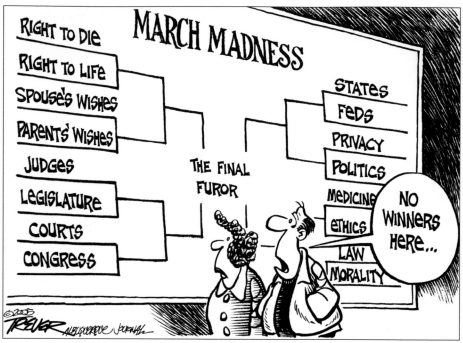

The cartoon bracket reads:

MARCH MADNESS

RIGHT TO DIE
RIGHT TO LIFE
SPOUSE'S WISHES
PARENTS' WISHES
JUDGES
LEGISLATURE
COURTS
CONGRESS

THE FINAL FUROR

STATES
FEDS
PRIVACY
POLITICS
MEDICINE
ETHICS
LAW
MORALITY

NO WINNERS HERE...

many years ago. It is slightly yellowed with age now, but I can still read it very clearly.

And a question occurs to me: Who, or what, is being assisted to commit suicide? Disabled or ill human beings, of course. But the medical profession itself is also committing suicide. True, the legal profession is rushing to assist us physicians to do so. But we can't put all the blame on lawyers and judges. They are only assisting in the lethal decision we physicians have made for ourselves.

Terri Schiavo, and those like her, aren't the only ones slowly dehydrated and starved to death. The medical profession itself is in the same unhappy situation. The process of starvation is already far advanced. But unlike Terri, there is still time to save the profession—if we start right away.

Quick! Start an IV. Begin an infusion of moral principles and ethical values. Restore medicine to its former healthy state of independent professionals dedicated to the wellbeing of individual patients, rather than mere technicians serving the economic interests of their employers or the state.

Heal and Never Kill

About 2400 years ago, Hippocrates told physicians to heal and never to kill. About 3200 years ago, the Bible told all of us, ". . . I have set before you life and death, blessings and curses. Now choose life, so that you and your children may live. . . ." As for me, I'll take these as my beacons to steer by. Others will check the news daily, so they can be guided by the latest court decision. It's your choice.

EVALUATING THE AUTHOR'S ARGUMENTS:

Stolinsky compares physician-assisted suicide to Nazi euthanasia practices. Why do you think he does this? Do you think this comparison strengthens or weakens his argument? Explain.

Hospice Helps the Dying

Patricia Ahern

"Hospice seeks to neither hasten nor prolong death; hospice seeks to give you the quality of life you want when facing your final days."

In the following viewpoint Patricia Ahern asserts that hospice enhances the quality of life of the dying in their final days and neither hastens nor prolongs death. Ahern says the American public and even those who work in the health-care field need to be better educated about what hospice is, how it can help, and its availability to people of all incomes. Ahern thinks that hospice provides an important end-of-life care option, which will become increasingly important as the baby boomer generation nears its elder years. Patricia Ahern is president and executive director of Rainbow Hospice in Park Ridge, Illinois.

AS YOU READ, CONSIDER THE FOLLOWING QUESTIONS:

1. According to Ahern, in a Canadian study of people with chronic diseases, two things were identified as having a positive effect on quality of life. What were these two things?
2. Name two of the myths that Ahern says must be dispelled about hospice.
3. According to Ahern, what fraction of all Medicare beneficiaries ever use their hospice benefit?

Patricia Ahern, "End of Life—Not End of Story," *Modern Healthcare,* vol. 37, June 18, 2007, p. 24. Copyright © 2007 Crain Communications, Inc. Reproduced by permission.

Our society is growing older by the day, and the number of aging adults will soon reach an all-time high. By 2030, about 20% of Americans will be 65 or older, up from the current 12%, the Census Bureau reported last year [2006]. In the not-too-distant future, the baby boomers will begin to think about how their lives will end, and hospice will loom ever larger in the healthcare provider landscape.

Hospice Enhances Quality of Life

A recent study published in the journal *Research in Nursing & Health*, looked at more than 400 Canadians between the ages of 60 and 99 with a variety of illnesses, including chronic lung and heart problems. According to the study, companionship and intimacy have a moderate to strong positive effect on quality of life and can even enhance it over time.

Those are the same values that are brought to bear every day in hospice care. Many organizations, including mine, customize care for each patient, helping them navigate through the turbulence of serious illness. As studies focus on quality of life in older age, we as end-of-life caregivers help to enable people to live with dignity and hope while coping with loss and the coming end of life.

Therapy dogs have been found to bring pleasure to patients in hospice.

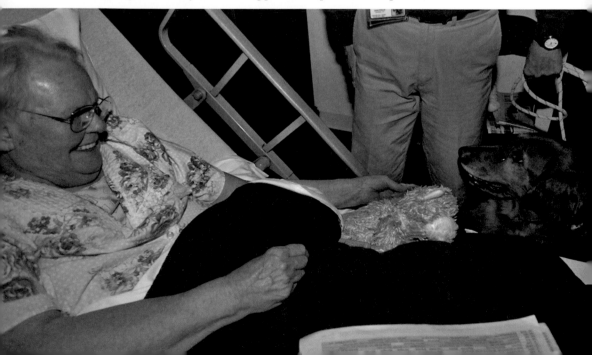

A very real advantage for hospice patients is the acute understanding of the limited time remaining and the support of an entire team, dedicated to adding life to the days they have left.

Americans Need to Be Educated About Hospice

End-of-life care is going to become transformed by the boomers, and hospice is going to play a major role in how this care is provided. And yet, the majority of Americans seem to be unaware of what hospice really means and what hospice care can provide a dying patient and his or her family. There is a need for overall education about hospice in the next decade.

First, we must dispel the myths about hospice, which run deep: Do you really die sooner in hospice care? Is hospice only for people with cancer? Is it only available at a hospital and is it unaffordable? Here's some clarification.

A 2007 study [reported in the *Journal of Pain and Symptom Management*] showed that many people actually live longer when receiving hospice care. Hospice seeks to neither hasten nor prolong death; hospice seeks to give you the quality of life you want when facing your final days.

Nationally, patients with cancer now represent less than half of those receiving hospice care. Hospice care is for any person who has a life-threatening or terminal illness.

Hospice care does not mean spending your final days in a hospital. Hospice is a philosophy of care and is brought to the patient and family wherever that may be. Hospice can be provided in an individual's home, nursing home, retirement community, prison or hospital. Some hospices may have inpatient units or a residence as options for the site of care.

Hospice is covered by Medicare, Medicaid and most private insurance companies. In cases when there is no insurance, many hospices have a sliding scale, self-pay rate or financial assistance program. The sad truth is that only one-third of all Medicare beneficiaries ever use their hospice benefit, which they paid for and deserve.

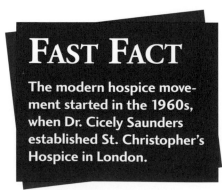

FAST FACT

The modern hospice movement started in the 1960s, when Dr. Cicely Saunders established St. Christopher's Hospice in London.

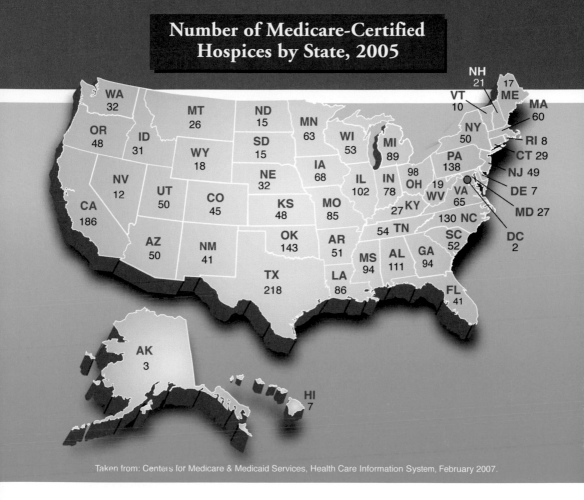

Number of Medicare-Certified Hospices by State, 2005

WA 32
OR 48
ID 31
MT 26
ND 15
MN 63
WI 53
MI 89
NH 21
VT 10
ME 17
MA 60
NY 50
RI 8
CT 29
NV 12
UT 50
WY 18
SD 15
NE 32
IA 68
IL 102
IN 78
OH 98
PA 138
NJ 49
CA 186
CO 45
KS 48
MO 85
KY 27
WV 19
VA 65
DE 7
MD 27
AZ 50
NM 41
OK 143
AR 51
TN 54
NC 130
SC 52
DC 2
TX 218
LA 86
MS 94
AL 111
GA 94
FL 41
AK 3
HI 7

Taken from: Centers for Medicare & Medicaid Services, Health Care Information System, February 2007.

While general myths about hospice are a concern, keeping everyone in the healthcare industry informed is another major concern for hospice. Many physicians are not aware of the Medicare and Medicaid benefit for hospice care and still [subscribe] to the belief that hospice is for cancer patients only. It is our job to educate physicians, nurses, social workers and other healthcare professionals about the benefits of hospice.

Finding Out About Hospice

The best way to find out about a hospice is to interview all the hospices in your area or to talk to someone you trust that is familiar with hospice. Resources for information about hospice care in your community include physicians, nurses and other healthcare professionals; social workers, clergy and other counselors; and local or state offices or departments on aging.

Baby boomers are wealthier than any prior generation and have different needs and greater expectations than their parents. Many seek out nutrition advice, care across the spectrum and personal trainers. They expect, with good reason, to live well past 70, and so, the quality of that longer life is now in the forefront of people's minds.

What does it mean for this new generation of Americans navigating end-of-life care options for their parents and ultimately for themselves?

Hospice Means Hope

When facing serious illness, many people learn that there is much to hope for and wish for in their lives. Hospice helps people achieve their goals and supports the family as they care for their loved one. A person in a hospice program may hope for comfort instead of cure, may hope for resolution with family members, may hope for a night out with their spouse or may hope for the opportunity to participate in a family celebration. Hospice helps to convert all this hope to reality.

Elder care is fast becoming an important issue for the aging baby boomers. Now is the time to educate and let people know what type of care is available so they can die with dignity and hope.

EVALUATING THE AUTHORS' ARGUMENTS:

In the viewpoint you just read, Patricia Ahern says it is a myth that people die sooner when they are in hospice. In the next viewpoint, Ron Panzer contends that people do die sooner in hospice. In your opinion, which of the two authors makes a more persuasive argument? Explain.

Hospice Hastens Death

Ron Panzer

"While many in hospice assert that they will neither hasten death nor prolong death, hospice staff around the country may misuse common end of life interventions to hasten death."

In the following viewpoint Ron Panzer contends that the hospice movement in the United States is really a front for those promoting euthanasia. Panzer details the history of the right-to-die movement and says that the first hospice in America was founded by a major euthanasia representative. Panzer questions the motives of hospice workers and claims that many people who receive hospice care have their lives cut short.

Ron Panzer is the president of the Hospice Patients Alliance, an organization that seeks to expose flaws in the hospice movement.

AS YOU READ, CONSIDER THE FOLLOWING QUESTIONS:
1. According to Panzer, the Euthanasia Society of America was formed in what city and in what year?
2. How does Panzer define the term *terminal sedation*?
3. According to the author, who was to be the "unworthy of life" victim of the Hospice of the Florida Suncoast?

Right to life organizations have been out-maneuvered by the so-called right to die organizations. How did this occur? We have to look at the history of the right to die organizations and then the answer will be clear.

The History of the Right to Die Movement

Before the Third Reich, before War II, the eugenics and euthanasia advocates were quite active in the U.S. The Euthanasia Society of America, formed in 1938 in New York, having failed in getting passage of laws legalizing euthanasia, changed its tactics. Realizing that the sanctity of life ethic was alive and well in the U.S., they sought a way to chip away at the bedrock blocking their way. Commissioning research to learn what phrases their dark agenda could be palatably sold to the American public, they came up with terms such as 'choice in dying,' 'dying well,' 'the right to die' and 'patient choice.'

In the 1960s they changed their name to Choice in Dying, choosing to focus on incrementally advancing the euthanasia agenda. Living wills, advanced directives, and do not resuscitate orders were successfully sold to the U.S. and accepted by the mainstream health care industry policymakers.

Simultaneous with the introduction of the living will and the advanced directives initiative, hospice care arrived on the scene, suggesting that we avoid aggressive acute hospital care when such interventions may be burdensome and intrusive for patients who are truly dying. Providing compassionate care to the terminally ill, relieving their suffering while allowing a natural death in its own timing . . . who could object?

FAST FACT

The Connecticut Hospice was the first hospice in the United States. It began providing services in March 1974.

Hospice Is Used as a Back Door to Euthanasia

What the public did not know is that the first hospice in our nation, the Connecticut Hospice, was founded by a major representative of the euthanasia movement, Florence Wald, MSN, who stated that assisted suicide should be available for just about any reason at all:

I'll tell you the way I see it, and I know that I differ from Cicely Saunders [founder of the hospice movement] who is very much against assisted suicide. I disagree with her view on the basis that there are cases in which either the pain or the debilitation the patient is experiencing is more than can be borne, whether it be economically, physically, emotionally, or socially. For this reason, I feel a range of options should be available to the patient, and this should include assisted suicide.

While many in hospice assert that they will neither hasten death nor prolong death, hospice staff around the country may misuse common end of life interventions to hasten death. Terminal sedation, a common intervention to relieve severe agitation at the end of life, can be misapplied to place patients into a medically-induced coma from which they are not allowed to recover. They die of dehydration while sleeping, thereby allowing for a 'pretty' and peaceful,' but unnatural death, i.e., murder.

Some believe that Terry Schiavo was moved into a hospice center so she could be euthanized.

Right to life organizations have traditionally viewed hospice as the rightful alternative to euthanasia and have ardently supported hospice services, and so they should, IF hospices remain loyal to the original hospice mission of the London-based Dame Cicely Saunders, the founder of the modern hospice movement. But the euthanasia advocates have always known that hospice could be used as the back door to legalization of euthanasia and/or physician-assisted suicide.

And that is what has been occurring throughout the U.S. We have families reporting their loved one was killed off outright within hospices, through inappropriate use of medications when there was no clinical need, resulting in the death of an otherwise non-dying patient. . . .

Euthanasia Permeates Hospice

The euthanasia advocates have taken over the national policymaking circles of the entire hospice industry. Doubt it? Well, remember the Euthanasia Society of America? It changed its name to Choice in Dying, which sounds great, but was clearly an early indication that the choice they really wanted to promote was the choice to have physician-assisted suicide and/or euthanasia.

Choice in Dying completed its mission, the nationwide acceptance of incremental changes in our attitude toward life, substituting a 'quality of life' ethic for the 'sanctity of life' ethic. Having done its job, it looked forward to the next step: the direct control of the hospice industry. Choice in Dying merged with the hospice industry coalition, Partnership for Caring, whose goal was the changing of state and federal laws to favor utilization of hospice. Partnership for Caring merged with Last Acts, one of the largest hospice coalitions in the world, funded by the Robert Woods Johnson Foundation, to become Last Acts Partnership. Many who have served as Last Acts Partnership's directors also serve on the National Hospice & Palliative Care Organization board.

For example, Mary Labyak, C.E.O. of the Hospice of the Florida Suncoast, served as secretary at the Partnership for Caring and is a prominent leader in the hospice industry, having served on the boards of Last Acts and the National Hospice & Palliative Care Organization.

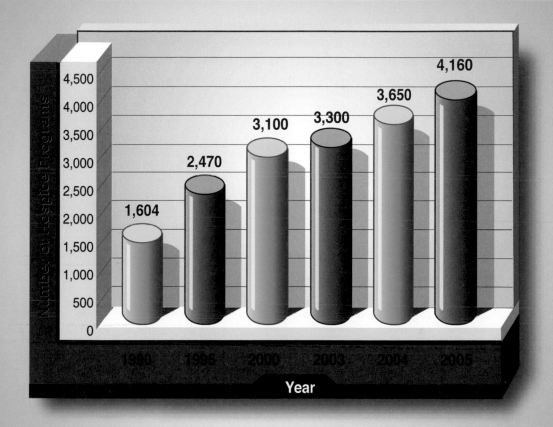

Taken from: National Hospice and Palliative Care Organization, November 2006.

It is Labyak's hospice, Hospice of the Florida Suncoast, which has actively participated in accepting a non-terminal patient, Terri Schiavo into the hospice, for the express purpose of euthanizing the 'unworthy of life' victim, Terri Schiavo.

Hospice Is Not Safe
Those who think hospice is the safe alternative to open euthanasia have been outfoxed. The euthanasia society has run circles around the well-meaning but naive right to lifers. So whether euthanasia is legalized openly or 'back-doored' through hospice, euthanasia is here, and it has been here for a long time. The National Right to Life Committee

has known about the hospice killings for years, yet has refused to expose these killings.

Is the right to life groups' stance on hospice consistent with its professed opposition to euthanasia? Only if it admits that the realities in hospice are mixed, and citizens of our nation need to remain vigilant in determining whether their loved one is receiving end of life care, or is receiving care that leads to the end of life at will, i.e., euthanasia.

EVALUATING THE AUTHOR'S ARGUMENTS:

Ron Panzer does not believe that hospice care in the United States is safe. What is the main point of his argument?

Chapter 3

What Happens After Death?

Customs involving burial of the dead are often closely tied to a culture's belief about afterlife.

The Bible Contains Reincarnation

Kevin Williams

"Reincarnation is a doctrine which can be accepted by every follower of Christ and should be a part of orthodox Christian doctrine."

In the following viewpoint Kevin Williams asserts that reincarnation was believed by many early Judeo-Christian leaders, references to it are contained in the Bible, and it is a concept that is compatible with Christianity. Williams says that Christians are generally confused about the difference between reincarnation, which is the rebirth of a person's spirit into a new body, and spiritual resurrection, which is a new spirit being created in an old body. Jesus himself taught about reincarnation, says Williams, but in A.D. 553 the Roman Catholic Church incorrectly declared it to be heretical.

Kevin Williams is an author and the owner of the Web site Near-Death Experiences and the Afterlife. (www.near-death.com).

AS YOU READ, CONSIDER THE FOLLOWING QUESTIONS:
1. According to Williams, what movie does the orthodox Christian doctrine of resurrection resemble?
2. Who does Williams contend was the first great father of the early orthodox church?
3. According to the author, Jesus defined for Nicodemus the difference between what two things?

In many documented near-death experiences (NDEs) involving Jesus, the concept of reincarnation appears. . . . One of the reasons many Christians reject the validity of near-death testimony is because they sometimes appear to conflict with their interpretation of Christian doctrines. But Christians are usually very surprised to learn that reincarnation was a doctrine once held by many early Christians. Not only that, as you will soon see there is overwhelming evidence in the Bible of Jesus himself teaching it. . . .

Christian Misconceptions

Many Christians have misconceptions about reincarnation. One particular misconception is that it means people don't inhabit heavenly realms between earth lives. The misconception is that people reincarnate immediately after death. It ignorantly assumes people will never be permanent residents of heavenly realms. But near-death testimony reveals these misconceptions to be just that—misconceptions. People are free to spend an "eternity of eternities" in afterlife realms before reincarnating to earth again. There is freedom of choice. This is because time, as we know it on Earth, does not exist in the afterlife realms as it does here. The ultimate purpose for reincarnation is for us to learn enough lessons and gain enough experience from earth lives that reincarnation is no longer necessary. Like a graduation. Reincarnation is not the goal. Eternal life means never having to die anymore. That is the goal—overcoming death and rebirth. Reincarnation is the method and means to attain this goal. . . .

A good understanding of reincarnation begins by understanding the ancient teachings on the subject and comparing them to what we know about NDEs. The following are teachings of the various ancient religions on reincarnation.

Resurrection Misunderstanding

For thousands of years, Christians believed that when a person dies their soul would sleep in the grave along with their corpse. This soul sleep continues until a time in the future known as the "last day" or also known as the "final judgment." This doctrine concerns a time when Jesus supposedly returns in the sky and clouds with the angels to awaken sleeping souls in the graves. Then all corpses will crawl out of their graves like in the movie "Night of the Living Dead." This doctrine is the orthodox

Christian doctrine called "resurrection" and it is the result of a misunderstanding of the higher teachings of Jesus concerning the reincarnation of the spirit into a new body and the real resurrection which is a spiritual rebirth or "awakening" within a person already alive. . . .

Resurrection of the Spirit

When Jesus began his ministry, many people wondered if he was the reincarnation of one of the prophets. Some people wondered the same thing concerning John the Baptist. And even Jesus affirmed to his disciples that John the Baptist was indeed the reincarnation of the prophet Elijah. Throughout his ministry, Jesus taught people about the true resurrection—a spiritual rebirth within a living person. Thus, when Jesus stated that he was the resurrection and the life, he was teaching them a radical new principle. It was a rebirth of the spirit—not into a new body—as when we are born from our mother's womb—but a rebirth of our spirit within the body we now inhabit. Jesus was distinguishing between what was already believed in those days concerning the afterlife and a new teaching concerning a spiritual change within us that can lead to liberation. He was making a distinction between "the resurrection of the body" (returning to life from physical death) and "the resurrection of the spirit" (returning to life from spiritual death). As you will soon see, this confusion concerning Jesus' teachings is documented in John 3 when Jesus had to explain to Nicodemus the difference between physical rebirth and spiritual rebirth. . . .

Early Reincarnation Teachings Have Been Destroyed

The first great Father of the early orthodox Church was Origen (A.D. 185–254) who was the first person since Paul to develop a system of theology around the teachings of Jesus. Origen was an ardent defender of pre-existence and reincarnation. Pre-existence is the religious concept of the soul as not being created at birth; rather the soul existed before birth in heaven or in a past life on earth. Origen taught that pre-existence is found in Hebrew scriptures and the teachings of Jesus. . . .

The doctrines of pre-existence and reincarnation existed as secret teachings of Jesus until they were declared a heresy by the Roman Church in 553 A.D. It was at this time that the Roman Church aggressively destroyed competing teachings and so-called heresies within the Church. Along with the destruction of unorthodox teachings came the destruction of Jews, Gnostics, and ultimately anyone who stood in the way of the Inquisition and Crusades. . . .

Biblical Examples of Reincarnation

There are many Bible verses that affirm the reality of reincarnation. We will examine some of them here.

The episode in the Bible where Jesus identified John the Baptist as the reincarnation of Elijah the prophet is one of the clearest statements which Jesus made concerning reincarnation.

> For all the prophets and the law have prophesied until John. And if you are willing to receive it, he is Elijah who was to come. (Matt. 11:13–14)

In the above passage, Jesus clearly identifies John the Baptist as the reincarnation of Elijah the prophet. Later in Matthew's gospel Jesus reiterates it.

> And the disciples asked him, saying, "Why then do the scribes say that Elijah must come first?"
>
> But he answered them and said, "Elijah indeed is to come and will restore all things. But I say to you that *Elijah has come already*, and they did not know him, but did to him whatever they wished. So also shall the Son of Man suffer at their hand."
>
> Then the disciples understood that *he had spoken of John the Baptist.* (Matt. 17:10–13)

In very explicit language, Jesus identified John the Baptist as the reincarnation of Elijah. Even the disciples of Jesus understood what Jesus was saying. This identification of John to be the reincarnation of Elijah is very important when it comes to Bible prophecy. By identifying John with Elijah, Jesus identified himself as the Messiah. The Hebrew scriptures mention specific signs that would precede the coming of the Messiah. One of them is that Elijah will return first. . . .

Being "Born Again"

One of the most controversial passages of scripture dealing with the doctrine of reincarnation is the conversation that Jesus had with Nicodemus, a Pharisee who believed in reincarnation (as all Pharisees did in those

Some people cite one of the gospels in claiming that Jesus identified John the Baptist as the reincarnation of the prophet Elijah.

days). The controversy, as it was with Nicodemus, has to do with the metaphor "born again" and what it means. Jesus uses the concept of rebirth to explain both physical rebirth (reincarnation) and spiritual rebirth (regeneration by the Holy Spirit). Jesus explains to Nicodemus:

> I tell you a truth, no one can see the kingdom of God unless he is born again. (John 3:3)

Jesus affirms that the way to heaven is through spiritual regeneration by the Holy Spirit. Although Nicodemus knew how people are reborn into the world through reincarnation, he couldn't understand how people are reborn into the kingdom of God through reincarnation. This confusion becomes apparent with Nicodemus' next statement:

> How can a person be born when he is old? Surely he cannot enter a second time into his mother's womb to be born! (John 3:4)

Nicodemus was confused about Jesus' use of the phrase "born again" when not used to describe physical rebirth (i.e., reincarnation). As an intelligent Pharisee, he was well aware that souls come from a past life to be born as babies. But he couldn't understand how a soul can get to heaven through physical rebirth. Because of this, Jesus explained to him the difference between physical rebirth and spiritual rebirth:

> I tell you the truth, no one can enter the kingdom of God unless he is born of water and the Spirit. Flesh gives birth to flesh, but the Spirit gives birth to spirit. (John 3:5–6)

FAST FACT

In a 2001 Gallup poll, 25 percent of Americans said they believed in reincarnation.

Jesus defined for Nicodemus the difference between physical rebirth (i.e., bodily reincarnation, "born of water") as all babies are born; and spiritual rebirth (i.e., spiritual resurrection, "born of the Spirit"). . . .

In Defense of Reincarnation

In conclusion, this Biblical defense of reincarnation leads to the following conclusions:

1. The religious concept of a massive worldwide reanimation of corpses at the end of time is a foreign concept originating from ancient Persia.
2. A massive worldwide reanimation of corpses seems bizarre, unnatural, and repulsive.
3. The few instances recorded in the Bible where corpses were reanimated were miracles. Doctors today bring people back from the dead with modern technology.
4. Reincarnation was widely believed by the people of Israel in the days of Jesus and by people all around the world.
5. All Hebrew and Christian scriptures support reincarnation: the Bible, the Dead Sea Scrolls, the Christian Gnostic gospels, the Torah, the Hebrew Bible, the Apocrypha, the Kabbalah and Zohar.
6. Many of the Biblical references to "resurrection" refer to spiritual regeneration while already physically alive instead of the reanimation of corpses on the so-called "Last Day."
7. *Reincarnation* is the rebirth of a person's spirit into a new body to be born again as an infant. *Resurrection* is the "spiritual awakening" of a living person's spirit by the power of the Holy Spirit.
8. The Bible records Jesus himself teaching reincarnation to his followers.
9. Early Christians in Jerusalem believed in reincarnation and taught it until it was declared a heresy by the Church of Rome.
10. Reincarnation has been a tenet in Orthodox Judaism for thousands of years and continues to this day.
11. The concept of reincarnation is supported by many near-death experiences including those where Jesus appears.
12. Reincarnation is a doctrine which can be accepted by every follower of Christ and should be a part of orthodox Christian doctrine.

EVALUATING THE AUTHORS' ARGUMENTS:

In the viewpoint you just read, Kevin Williams says that reincarnation is compatible with Christianity. In the next viewpoint the author contends that reincarnation is not compatible with Christianity. Are there any similarities between the two authors in the way they support their contentions?

Reincarnation Is Not in the Bible

Ernest Valea

> "No matter how many attempts are made today to find texts in the Bible or in the history of the Church that would allegedly teach reincarnation, they are all doomed to remain flawed."

In the following viewpoint Ernest Valea contends that reincarnation is antithetical to Christian beliefs and teachings. Valea refutes the theory that some biblical texts refer to reincarnation. For instance, Valea says that John the Baptist was not a reincarnation of Elijah, and Jesus did not teach Nicodemus about reincarnation. According to Valea, reincarnation compromises God's sovereignty over creation and represents a threat to the very essence of Christianity.

Ernest Valea is a theologian, author, and the owner of the Web site Comparative Religion (www.comparativereligion.com).

AS YOU READ, CONSIDER THE FOLLOWING QUESTIONS:

1. According to Valea, the prophecy of the return of Elijah appears in what book of the Old Testament?

Ernest Valea, "Reincarnation: Its Meaning and Consequences: Reincarnation and Christianity," Comparativereligion.com, 1999–2007. Reproduced by permission.

2. When they were traveling in the wilderness, God punished the Israelites for speaking against both Him and Moses. According to Valea, what was God's solution after the Israelites recognized their sin and ask for a saving solution?
3. Valea says an extreme application of reincarnationist convictions could lead to adopting a detached stand against what?

Today's religious syncretism [combination of beliefs] not only accepts reincarnation as one of its basic doctrines but also tries to prove that it can be found in the Bible and that it was accepted by the early Church. We will therefore analyze the basic texts in the Bible which are claimed to imply belief in reincarnation, examine the position of some important Church fathers who are said to have accepted it, and emphasize the basic antagonism of this doctrine with Christian teaching.

Some Biblical Texts Seem to Imply Reincarnation
The most "convincing" texts of this kind are the following:
1. Matthew 11,14 and 17,12–13, concerning the identity of John the Baptist;
2. John 9,2, "Who sinned, this man or his parents, that he was born blind?";
3. John 3,3, "No one can see the kingdom of God unless he is born again";
4. James 3,6, "the wheel of nature";
5. Galatians 6,7, "A man reaps what he sows";
6. Matthew 26,52, "all who draw the sword will die by the sword";
7. Revelation 13,10, "If anyone is to go into captivity, into captivity he will go. If anyone is to be killed with the sword, with the sword he will be killed."

The Same Spirit, but Not the Same Soul
The first text concerns the identity of John the Baptist, supposed to be the reincarnation of the prophet Elijah. In *Matthew* 11,14 Jesus says: "And if you are willing to accept it, he (John the Baptist) is the Elijah who was to come." In the same Gospel, while answering the

apostles about the coming of Elijah, Jesus told them: "But I tell you, Elijah has already come, and they did not recognize him, but have done to him everything they wished. In the same way the Son of Man is going to suffer at their hands." The commentary adds: "Then the disciples understood that he was talking to them about John the Baptist" (*Matthew* 17,12–13; see also *Mark* 9,12–13).

At first sight, it may seem that these verses imply the reincarnation of the prophet Elijah as John the Baptist. The prophecy of the return of Elijah appears in the last verses of the Old Testament, in the book of the prophet *Malachi* (3,1; 4,5–6): "See, I will send you the prophet Elijah before that great and dreadful day of the Lord comes." In *Luke* 1,17 an angel announces the fulfillment of this prophecy at the birth of John the Baptist: "And he will go on before the Lord, in the spirit and power of Elijah, to turn the hearts of the fathers to their children and the disobedient to the wisdom of the righteous—to make ready a people prepared for the Lord." What could be the meaning of the words "in the spirit and power of Elijah"?

First we must be aware that the Jews viewed 'spirit' and 'soul' as quite different things. The human person has a soul which will live on after physical death. The spirit is a kind of driving force, a motivation that makes people behave in one way or another. When a group

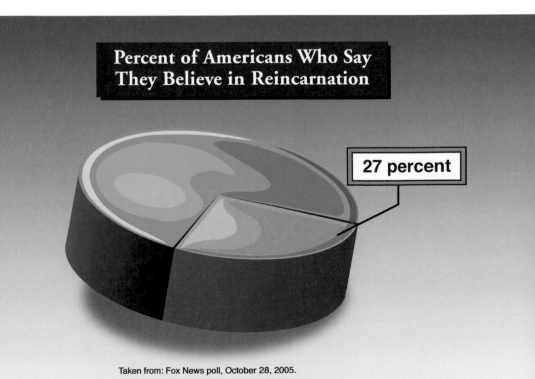

Percent of Americans Who Say They Believe in Reincarnation

27 percent

Taken from: Fox News poll, October 28, 2005.

of people are working to fulfill a common goal, they are said to be in the same spirit. Second, the text does not say that John the Baptist will go "in the soul of Elijah," but "in the spirit of Elijah." This means that John the Baptist and Elijah had the same "team spirit," not that one was the reincarnation of the other. John the Baptist was rather a kind of Elijah, a prophet who had to repeat the mission of Elijah in a similar context. The same as Elijah did nine centuries before him, John the Baptist had to suffer persecution from the royal house of Israel and act in the context of the spiritual degeneration of the Jewish nation. John had the same spiritual mission as the prophet Elijah, but not the same soul or self. For this reason the expression "in the spirit and power of Elijah" should not be interpreted as meaning the reincarnation of a person, but as a necessary repetition of a well-known episode in the history of Israel. . . .

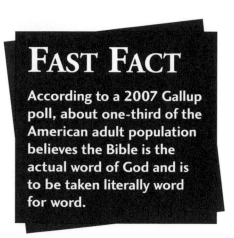

FAST FACT

According to a 2007 Gallup poll, about one-third of the American adult population believes the Bible is the actual word of God and is to be taken literally word for word.

Jesus Taught Spiritual Rebirth, Not Reincarnation

In the *Gospel According to John* Jesus said to Nicodemus: "I tell you the truth, no one can see the kingdom of God unless he is born again" (*John* 3,3). Out of its context, this verse seems to suggest that reincarnation is the only possibility for attaining spiritual perfection and admission into the "kingdom of God." Nicodemus' following question indicates that he understood by these words a kind of physical rebirth in this life, and not classic reincarnation: "How can a man be born when he is old? Surely he cannot enter a second time into his mother's womb to be born!" (v. 4). Jesus rejected the idea of physical rebirth and explained man's need for *spiritual rebirth*, during this life, in order to be admitted into God's kingdom in the afterlife.

Jesus further explained the meaning of his words by referring to a well-known episode in Israel's history: "Just as Moses lifted up the snake in the desert, so the Son of Man must be lifted up" (*John* 3,14).

That episode occurred while the Israelites were travelling in the wilderness toward the Promised Land under the command of Moses (see *Numbers* 21, 4–9). They spoke against God and against Moses, and God punished them by sending poisonous snakes against them. Grasping the gravity of the situation, they recognized their sin and asked for a saving solution. God's solution was that Moses had to make a bronze copy of such a snake and put it up on a pole. Those who had been bitten by a snake had to look at this bronze snake, believing that this symbol represented their salvation, and so were healed. Coming back to the connection Jesus made between that episode and his teaching, he said: "Just as Moses lifted up the snake in the desert, so the Son of Man must be lifted up, that everyone who believes in him may have eternal life" (*John* 3,14–15). In other words, as Moses lifted up the bronze snake 13 centuries earlier, in the same way was Jesus to be lifted up on the cross, in order to be the only antidote to the deadly bite of sin. As the Jews had to believe that the bronze snake was their salvation from death, the same way Nicodemus, his generation and the entire world had to believe that Jesus' sacrifice on

Some believe that reincarnation in the Bible is actually referring to the kind of spiritual rebirth experienced through religious rites like baptism.

the cross is the perfect solution provided by God for the sins of the world. Therefore the kind of rebirth Jesus was teaching was not the Eastern concept of reincarnation but a spiritual rebirth that any human can experience in this life. . . .

As can be observed, in all situations where "Biblical proofs" for reincarnation are claimed, the context is always ignored. Other passages used as proofs of reincarnationist beliefs mean, in fact, the existence of Christ prior to his human birth (*John* 8,58), the continuity of the souls' existence after death (*John* 5,28–29; *Luke* 16,22–23; *2 Corinthians* 5,1), or the spiritual rebirth of believers in their present life (*Titus* 3,5: *I Peter* 1,23), without giving any plausible indication for reincarnation.

No Proof of a Biblical Revision

Another hypothesis is that the Bible contained many passages teaching reincarnation in an alleged initial form, but they were suppressed by the clergy at the fifth ecumenical council, held in Constantinople in the year AD 553. The reason for this would have been the spiritual immaturity of the Christians, who could not grasp the doctrine at that time, or the desire of the clergy to manipulate the masses. However, there is no proof that such "purification" of the Biblical text has ever occurred. The existing manuscripts, many of them older than AD 553, do not show differences from the text we use today. There are enough reasons to accept that the New Testament was not written later than the first century AD. . . .

Reincarnation Is Inconsistent with Christianity

The idea of reincarnation has never been accepted by Christianity because it undermines its basic tenets. First, it compromises God's sovereignty over creation, transforming him into a helpless spectator of the human tragedy. But since he is sovereign and omnipotent over creation, God can punish evil and will do it perfectly well at the end of history (see *Matthew* 25,31–46: *Revelation* 20,10–15). There is no need for the impersonal law of karma and for reincarnation to play this role.

Second, belief in reincarnation may affect one's understanding of morality and motivation for moral living. An extreme application of reincarnationist convictions could lead to adopting a detached stand to crime, theft and other social plagues. They could be considered nothing else but normal debts to be paid by their victims, which originated in previous lives.

Third, reincarnation represents a threat to the very essence of Christianity: the need for Christ's redemptive sacrifice for our sins. If we are to pay for the consequences of our sins ourselves in further lives and attain salvation through our own efforts, the sacrifice of Christ becomes useless and absurd. It wouldn't be the only way back to God, but only a stupid accident of history. In this case Christianity would be a mere form of Hindu Bhakti-Yoga.

As result, no matter how many attempts are made today to find texts in the Bible or in the history of the Church that would allegedly teach reincarnation, they are all doomed to remain flawed.

EVALUATING THE AUTHORS' ARGUMENTS:

Both Ernest Valea, the author of the viewpoint you just read, and Kevin Williams, the author of the previous viewpoint, use Bible verses to support their arguments. Are there any Bible verses that appear in both viewpoints? Which author do you think uses Bible verses more effectively and why?

There Is an Afterlife

Deepak Chopra

"We have to shift our notion of the afterlife from being a place to being a state of awareness. Once we do that, life after death becomes much more plausible."

In the following viewpoint Deepak Chopra contends that there is an afterlife, but it's not a place that we arrive at; rather, it is an altered state of awareness. Chopra says it is possible to ask rational, nonreligious questions about the afterlife and provide proof of its existence. But, says Chopra, scientists like Michael Shermer tend to shy away from studying consciousness, the soul, or life after death because these phenomena "seem" unreal. Chopra believes the afterlife is real. He contends that the mind exists separate from the body and that after our bodies die, our minds persist within the universe, but they just move to a different state of awareness. Deepak Chopra is an author and spiritual speaker.

AS YOU READ, CONSIDER THE FOLLOWING QUESTIONS:

1. According to Chopra, people who return from the dead in Tibet are known as what?
2. Chopra contends that after we die, personality and memory begin to fade, but what sense remains?
3. According to the author, what is the name of the scientist at Boeing's aerospace laboratory in Seattle who provided a link between the two models of mind and matter?

Deepak Chopra, "Taking the Afterlife Seriously," Skeptic.com, January 2007. Reproduced by permission.

[W]illiam Shakespeare's character] Hamlet refers to death as "the undiscovered country from whose bourne no traveler returns." For all intents and purposes, this argument has sufficed for materialists ever since. But people do cross the boundary between life and death only to return—the number of near-death experiences is many thousands by now. . . . The existence of studies in which people do not have such experiences seems irrelevant. I can offer experiments where people can't identify the notes of the musical scale, but that doesn't mean perfect pitch is an illusion.

I was particularly interested in the resemblance between modern near-death experiences and those reported for hundreds of years in Tibet. People who return from the dead in that culture are known as delogs, and what they experience isn't a Christian heaven or hell—in this country 90 percent of near-death experiences, by the way, are positive—but the complex layers of the Buddhist Bardo. In our society heaven is generally reported by those who have near-death experiences as being like

A young girl draws a picture of what she claims to have seen during a near-death experience.

green pastures or blue skies; children tend to report a child's heaven populated by scampering lambs and other baby animals.

Perceptions of the Afterlife

This made me realize that Hamlet was right to call death an undiscovered country, not because the living cannot reach it but because heaven's geography keeps shifting. If we look at how various cultures perceive the afterlife, there are roughly seven categories:

1. Paradise: Your soul finds itself in a perfected world surrounding God. You go to Paradise as a reward and never leave. (If you are bad, you go to Satan's home and never leave it.)
2. The Godhead: Your soul returns to God, but not in any particular place. You discover the location of God as a timeless state infused with his presence
3. The Spirit World: Your soul rests in a realm of departed spirits. You are drawn back to those you loved in this life. Or you rejoin your ancestors, who are gathered with the great Spirit.
4. Transcendence: Your soul performs a vanishing act in which a person dissolves, either quickly or gradually. The pure soul rejoins the sea of consciousness from which it was born.
5. Transmigration (or Metempsychosis): Your soul is caught in the cycle of rebirth. Depending on one's karma, each soul rises or falls from lower to higher life forms—and even may be reborn in objects. The cycle continues eternally until your soul escapes through higher realization.
6. Awakening: Your soul arrives in the light. You see with complete clarity for the first time, realizing the truth of existence that was masked by being in a physical body.
7. Dissolution: Eternity is nothingness. As the chemical components of your body return to basic atoms and molecules, the consciousness created by the brain disappears completely. You are no more.

There is no common denominator here except one: consciousness itself. We have to shift our notion of the afterlife from being a place to being a state of awareness. Once we do that, life after death becomes much more plausible. Instead of arguing over religious beliefs, we can ask rational questions:

- Can consciousness survive the body's death?
- Is there mind outside the brain?
- Can we know the states of consciousness that belong to the afterlife without dying?
- Does consciousness have a basis outside time and space?

The Stages of the Afterlife

To me these are rational questions, and we can devise experiments to answer them. But before going into that, the issue most people want to settle is "What happens after we die?" Since this remains such a pressing question, let me offer the evidence that surfaced when I looked at cultures East and West. Leaving aside the place a

FAST FACT

In fiscal year 2006, the National Institutes of Health spent $136 million on research into the connection between the mind and the body.

person might go to (my position is that there is no "where" after death; everything is protected in consciousness, including heaven and hell), the afterlife appears to unfold in the following stages:

1. The physical body stops functioning. The dying person may not be aware of this but eventually knows that it occurred.
2. The physical world vanishes. This can happen by degrees; there can be a sense of floating upward or of looking down on familiar places as they recede.
3. The dying person feels lighter, suddenly freed of limitation.
4. The mind and sometimes the senses continue to operate. Gradually, however, what is perceived is non-physical.
5. A presence grows that is felt to be divine. This presence can be clothed in a light or in the body of angels or gods. The presence can communicate to the dying person.
6. Personality and memory begin to fade, but the sense of "I" remains.
7. This "I" has an overwhelming sense of moving on to another phase of existence.

As much as possible I have eliminated religious wording here because the persistence of consciousness has to be universal. It can't depend on specific beliefs, which change over time and from place to place. . . .

Scientists Do Not Like to Study the Afterlife

Right now there are many reasons why science is reluctant to test any of these propositions about the survival of consciousness. First and foremost is the ideology of materialism. [scientist and Skeptics Society director Michael] Shermer . . . [and] thousands of actual scientists . . . see the world entirely in material terms. For them, consciousness is as alien as the soul. Both are invisible, immaterial, and unmeasurable and therefore ipso facto unreal. By these standards virtual photons should also be unreal, but they aren't. . . . Other reasons include peer pressure—i.e., ridicule—even when a researcher is brilliant and scrupulous to the nth degree. Lack of funding is a problem, naturally, and above all there is the time-honored antithesis between science and religion. In an either/or world, it's hard to convince the religionists that rationality has a spiritual place or the scientists that your research isn't just a stalking horse for the Bible—see the recent social debate over Intelligent Design where neither side was willing to see the slightest merit in the other.

"Willing" the Lights to Move

None of these obstacles, however, has proven insurmountable. Let me offer some highlights in the research devoted to answering the most crucial questions about the possibility of life after death:

My core argument is based on consciousness being a field, like matter and energy fields, that we are all imbedded in, whether here and now or after death. It would help us greatly if our minds could alter the field. Then we would have a link between the two models of mind and matter. Such a link was provided by Helmut Schmidt, a researcher working for Boeing's aerospace laboratory in Seattle. Beginning in the mid-Sixties, Schmidt set out to construct a series of "quantum machines" that could emit random signals, with the aim of seeing if ordinary people could alter those signals using nothing more than their minds. The first machine detected radioactive decay from Strontium-90; each electron that was given off lit up either a red, blue, yellow, or green light. Schmidt asked ordinary people to predict, with the press of a button, which light would be illuminated next.

At first no one performed better than random, or 25 percent, in picking one of the four lights. Then Schmidt hit on the idea of using

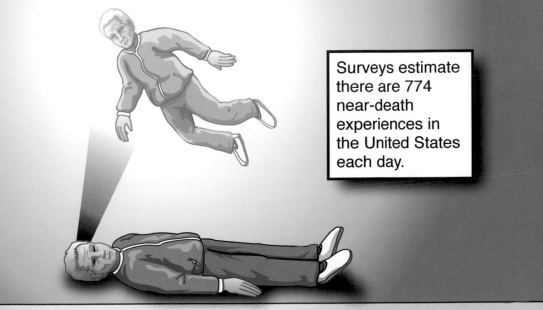

Near-Death Experiences

Surveys estimate there are 774 near-death experiences in the United States each day.

Taken from: Near Death Experience Research Foundation. www.nderf.org/.

psychics instead, and his first results were encouraging: they guessed the correct light 27 percent of the time. But he didn't know if this was a matter of clairvoyance—seeing the result before it happened—or something more active, actually changing the random pattern of electrons being emitted.

So he built a second machine that generated only two signals, call them plus and minus. A circle of lights was set up, and if the machine generated a plus, a light would come on in the clockwise direction while a minus would make one light up in the counter-clockwise direction. Left to itself, the machine would light up an equal number of pluses and minuses; what Schmidt wanted his subjects to do was to will the lights to move clockwise only. He found two subjects who had remarkable success. One could get the lights to move clockwise 52.5 percent of the time. An increase of 2.5 percent over randomness doesn't sound dramatic, but Schmidt calculated that the odds were 10 million to one against the same thing occurring by chance. The other subject was just as successful, but oddly enough, he couldn't make the lights move clockwise. Hard as he tried, they moved counter-clockwise, yet with the same deviation from randomness. Later experiments with new subjects raised the success rate to 54 percent, although the strange anomaly that the machine would go in the wrong direction, often persisted. (No explanation was ever found for this.) In effect, Schmidt was proving that an observer can change activity in the quantum field using the mind alone. . . .

The Burden of Proof

Can it be that the universe is organic, holistic, and aware? I am perfectly willing to accept Shermer's declaration that the burden of proof lies with those who claim this rather than with skeptics. But logically that's not actually true. We cannot prove that the universe *doesn't* have a mind, because we aren't mindless. Even when we declare that atoms and molecules act mindlessly, that is a mental statement. Nobody has ever experienced mindlessness; therefore we have nothing to base it on, just as a fish has nothing but wetness to base its reality on—dryness is a theological fancy under the sea.

EVALUATING THE AUTHORS' ARGUMENTS:

In the viewpoint you just read, Deepak Chopra uses scientific evidence to support his argument that there is life after death. In the next viewpoint, Michael Shermer also uses scientific evidence to support his argument that life after death does not exist. In your opinion, which viewpoint do you think the science supports? Are there some things that science cannot prove? Explain.

Viewpoint

4

No One Knows What Happens After Death

Michael Shermer

"Of the 100 billion people born before the six billion living today, every one of them has died and not one has returned to confirm for us beyond a reasonable doubt that there is life after death."

In the following viewpoint Michael Shermer contends that no one knows what happens after we die, but scientific evidence doesn't suggest that anything lives on after death. Shermer is skeptical and cynical toward people who believe there is an afterlife, including Deepak Chopra. Shermer presents research from various scientists that shows that near-death experiences, out-of-body experiences, and other phenomena that seem to suggest there is an afterlife are all just caused by chemicals in the brain. There is no afterlife, says Shermer; there is only the here and now.

Michael Shermer is the founding publisher of *Skeptic* magazine and the director of the Skeptics Society.

AS YOU READ, CONSIDER THE FOLLOWING QUESTIONS:

1. According to Shermer, what is the ancient Hebrew word for "soul"?

Michael Shermer, "Taking the Afterlife Seriously," Skeptic.com, January 2007. Reproduced by permission.

I once saw a bumper sticker that read:

Militant Agnostic: I Don't Know and You Don't Either.

This is my position on the afterlife: I don't know and you don't either. If we knew for certain that there is an afterlife, we would not fear death as we do, we would not mourn quite so agonizingly the death of loved ones, and there would be no need to engage in debates on the subject.

Because no one knows for sure what happens after we die, we deal with the topic in diverse ways through religion, literature, poetry, science, and even humor. . . .

Since I am a scientist and claims are made that there is scientific evidence for life after death, let us analyze the data for that doubtful future date, and consider what its possibility may mean for our present state.

Twenty-one Grams: The Nature of the Soul

What is it that supposedly survives the death of the physical body? The soul. There are about as many different understandings of the nature of the soul as there are religions and spiritual movements. The general belief is that *the soul is a conscious ethereal substance that is the unique essence of a living being that survives its incarnation in flesh.*

The ancient Hebrew word for soul is *nephesh,* or "life" or "vital breath"; the Greek word for soul is *psyche,* or "mind"; and the Roman Latin word for soul is *anima,* or "spirit" or "breath." The soul is the essence that breathes life into flesh, animates us, gives us our vital spirit. Given the lack of knowledge about the natural world at the time these concepts were first formed, it is not surprising these ancient peoples reached for such ephemeral metaphors as mind, breath, and spirit. One moment a little dog is barking, prancing, and wagging its tail, and in the next moment it is a lump of inert flesh. What happened in that moment?

In 1907 a Massachusetts physician named Duncan MacDougall tried to find out by weighing six dying patients before and after their death. He reported in the medical journal *American Medicine* that there was a 21-gram difference. Even though his measurements were crude and varying, and no one has been able to replicate his findings, it has nonetheless grown to urban legendary status as the weight of the soul. The implication is that the soul is a thing that can be weighed. Is it? . . .

Because the brain does not perceive itself, it imputes mental activity to a separate source—hallucinations of preternatural entities such as ghosts, angels, and aliens are perceived as actual beings; out-of-body and near-death experiences are sensed as external events instead of internal states. Likewise, the neural pattern of information that is our memories and personality—our "self"—is sensed as a soul. In this sense, the soul is an illusion.

FAST FACT

According to a 2005 Gallup poll, about three out of four Americans profess at least one paranormal belief. The most popular is extrasensory perception (ESP), mentioned by 41 percent, followed closely by a belief in haunted houses (37 percent).

Evidence of an Afterlife?

There are many scientistic scenarios for how we might cheat death that I have evaluated in my books and columns, but here I wish to focus on the latest claim for evidence of an afterlife presented in Deepak Chopra's 2006 book, *Life After Death: Burden of Proof.* According to Chopra, there are six lines of evidence that convince him that the soul is real and eternal:

1. Near-Death Experiences and Altered States of Consciousness. . . .
2. ESP and Evidence of Mind. . . .
3. Quantum Consciousness. . . .
4. Psychic Mediumship and Talking to the Dead. . . .
5. Prayer and Healing Studies. . . .
6. Information Fields, Morphic Resonance, and the Universal Life Force. . . .

For Deepak Chopra, these six lines of scientific evidence point to something already described thousands of years ago by the *rishis*, or sages of Vedic India, first spiritual leaders of Hinduism. "The rishis believed that knowledge wasn't external to the knower but woven inside consciousness. Thus they had no need for an external God to solve the riddle of life and death," Chopra explains. Our essence is what the rishis called *Atman*, and what we call the soul. "Soul and Atman are a spark of the divine, the invisible component that brings God's presence into flesh and blood. The biggest difference between them is that in Vedanta the soul isn't separate from God. Unlike the Christian soul, Atman cannot come from God or return to him. There is unity between the human and the divine."

I confess that my Western scientific worldview makes it exceedingly (and often frustratingly) difficult for me to truly grasp what Deepak is talking about. . . .

But near as I can figure this is what he is saying. The universe is one giant conscious information field of timeless energy of which all of us are a part. Life is simply a temporary incarnation of this eternal field of consciousness, whose properties, he says, include: "The field works as a whole. It correlates distant events instantly. It remembers all events. It exists beyond time and space. It creates entirely within itself. Its creation grows and expands in an evolutionary direction. It is conscious." . . .

In Chopra's theory of the afterlife, birth and death are merely transitions to and from different manifestations of consciousness. "Without death there can be no present moment, for the last moment has to die to make the next one possible." Thus, he deduces, "We live in an endlessly re-created universe." There is no need to fear death, because "Death isn't about what I possess but about what I can become.". . .

It Is All Just Brain Chemistry

Okay, back to earth. Here is the reality. It has been estimated that in the last 50,000 years about 106 billion humans were born. Of the 100 billion people born before the six billion living today, every one of them has died and not one has returned to confirm for us beyond a reasonable doubt that there is life after death. This data set does not bode well for promises of immortality and claims for an afterlife. But let's review them one by one.

Five centuries ago demons haunted our world, with incubi and succubi tormenting their victims as they lay asleep in their beds. Two centuries ago spirits haunted our world, with ghosts and ghouls harassing their sufferers all hours of the night. Last century aliens haunted our world, with grays and greens abducting captives out of their beds and whisking them away for probing and prodding. Today people are experiencing near-death and out-of-body experiences, floating above their bodies, out of their bedrooms, and even off the planet into space.

What is going on here? Are these elusive creatures and mysterious phenomena in our world or in our minds? New evidence indicates

Those who don't believe in an afterlife see individual existence ending with the death of the body.

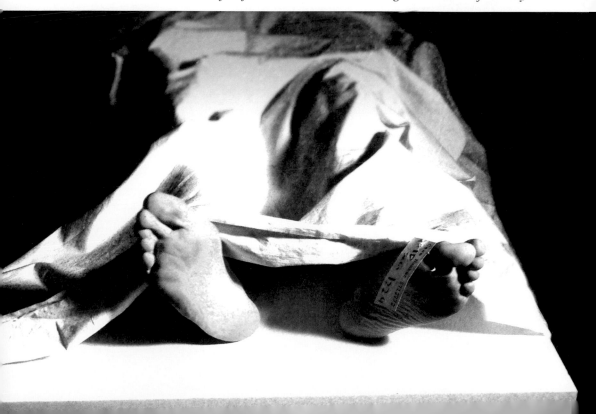

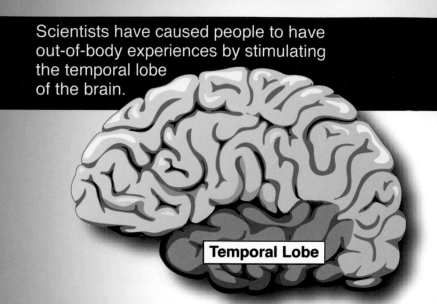

Manipulating the Brain

Scientists have caused people to have out-of-body experiences by stimulating the temporal lobe of the brain.

Temporal Lobe

that they are, in fact, a product of the brain. Neuroscientist Michael Persinger, in his laboratory at Laurentian University in Sudbury, Canada, for example, can induce all of these experiences in subjects by subjecting their temporal lobes to patterns of magnetic fields. I tried it and had a mild out-of-body experience.

Similarly, the September 19, 2002 issue of *Nature*, reported that the Swiss neuroscientist Olaf Blanke and his colleagues discovered that they could bring about out-of-body experiences (OBEs) through electrical stimulation of the right angular gyrus in the temporal lobe of a 43-year old woman suffering from severe epileptic seizures. In initial mild stimulations she reported "sinking into the bed" or "falling from a height." More intense stimulation led her to "see myself lying in bed, from above, but I only see my legs and lower trunk." Another stimulation induced "an instantaneous feeling of 'lightness' and 'floating' about two meters above the bed, close to the ceiling.". . .

Sometimes trauma can trigger such experiences. The December 2001 issue of *Lancet* published a Dutch study in which of 344 cardiac patients resuscitated from clinical death, 12 percent reported near-death experiences (NDEs), where they floated above their bodies and saw a light at the end of a tunnel. Some even described speaking to dead relatives.

The general explanation for all of these phenomena is that since our normal experience is of stimuli coming into the brain from the outside, when a part of the brain abnormally generates these illusions, another part of the brain interprets them as external events. Hence, the abnormal is thought to be the paranormal. In reality, it is just brain chemistry. . . .

The "Here and Now" Is What Is Important

So where does this leave us? I am, by temperament, a sanguine person, so I really hate to douse the flame of that doubtful future date with the cold water of skepticism in this present state. But I care what is actually true even more than what I hope is true, and these are the facts as I understand them to be. . . .

Where is paradise? It is here. It is now. It is within us and without us. It is in our thoughts and in our actions. It is in our lives and in our loves. It is in our families and in our friends. It is in our communities and in our world. It is in the courage of our convictions and in the character of our souls.

Hope springs eternal, even if life is not.

> **EVALUATING THE AUTHORS' ARGUMENTS:**
>
> In the viewpoint you just read, Michael Shermer argues against the existence of an afterlife. Within his argument Shermer describes the opposing viewpoint—that there is an afterlife—as it is presented by Deepak Chopra. Why do you think he does this? Do you think he could make his argument without describing the opposing viewpoint? Explain.

The Body Is Resurrected After Death

John F. Kavanaugh

> *"If there is to be personal immortality, there must be a reunification of the human soul with the body it informed and energized."*

In the following viewpoint John F. Kavanaugh asserts that after death the body is resurrected because the soul is incomplete without the body. The "essence" that makes each person unique, claims Kavanaugh, comes from the combination of a soul and a body. Kavanaugh believes that the resurrected body is in the form of a completed person, so the bodies of children who die are resurrected as fully grown adults. Elderly people are not resurrected in their aged bodies, but rather in their adult bodies at the prime of their life.

John F. Kavanaugh writes a regular column for *America* magazine. He is a Catholic priest and a professor of philosophy at St. Louis University.

AS YOU READ, CONSIDER THE FOLLOWING QUESTIONS:

1. According to Kavanaugh, how much of the human genome is shared with many plants? Up to how much is shared with other animals?

2. Those who believe in the theory of "transmigration" believe
   their soul ends up where, according to the author?
3. According to Kavanaugh, in what piece of writing did St.
   Thomas Aquinas conjecture that the soul bestows on the
   human body something glorious and that the raised body will
   be all it was meant to be?

U nder the influence of St. Thomas Aquinas, I hold that a "soul"
is a unifying formative source of any living being's activities
and purpose. Thus each individual plant or tree has a soul, a
formative cause of its integrated development in its life activities of
growth, healing and reproduction. Of a different order than these
"vegetative" souls, there are the "sensitive" souls that inform and inte-
grate the lives of animals. In addition to exhibiting the activities of
lowly plants, animals are endowed with powers of startling local motion
and a splendid array of cognitive and conative activities in their external and internal sensations.

The Soul Drives the Body and Creates Self-Awareness

Among animals, however, there are personal animals (embodied persons, rational animals, human beings) that have endowments or capacities for an astounding range of action in the world, from the creation
of cultural artifacts, to personal expression, to self-knowledge, self-
ownership and the capacity to give oneself away in freedom. These
capacities are astounding not only because we share 30 percent of our
genome with many plants and up to 98 percent with some other animals but also because self-consciousness and the reflexive awareness
that makes it all possible are inexplicable in materialistic accounts.
That is why it is called the "hard problem of consciousness." Some
materialists deny even that we are self-conscious; the more honest
acknowledge that we do indeed have self-consciousness, though we
cannot yet adequately explain it.

Like Aquinas, I believe that reflexive consciousness, or the intellect
that knows itself in knowing, will never be explained by material
causality. It is an immaterial or spiritual power that enables us to per-
form all the spiritual acts of love, freedom, rights claims, autonomy

commitment, faith, hope or love. (A full argument for this claim requires more than this column's space.) The reflexive consciousness of the intellect is not reducible to the organism but, in humans, can be expressed only through the organism, with its splendid brain. The person John Kavanaugh is the unified being who acts. I am not a soul, but my soul is the informing and integrating source of all my actions.

The question has therefore been asked, by countless philosophers and sometimes even ordinary people: What happens to John's soul when he dies? His soul's distinctly personal endowments are not reduced to matter. The material organism dies and corrupts. What about his soul?

After Death the Soul and the Body Reunite

As it turns out, Aquinas offers an account of the "afterlife" that is quite different from those of other thinkers. Some philosophers opined that the separated soul somehow becomes part of the Absolute or God, losing its individuality. Other traditions proposed a theory of transmigration: that the soul might travel to some other, usually newly conceived body.

For Aquinas, these options were unsatisfactory. They might insure the immortality of the soul, but certainly not the immortality of the person John Kavanaugh. The human soul is uniquely related to the human person, a personal body. Without the body, the human soul is incomplete. If there is to be personal immortality, there must somehow be a personalized body. Do I not need my body to be who I am, to have my memories and relations, to express my unique personhood?

Thus St. Thomas saw the strategic opening of his philosophy to the Christian belief in the resurrection of the body, a glorified body. Ultimately, if there is to be personal immortality, there must be a reunification of the human soul with the body it informed and energized. It cannot be the physical body in its transitional stages, but a fully realized body of that individual person. It might exhibit some properties of organic bodies but none of its limits. Like the risen Lord, who seemed to pass through doors, could be recognized and could even exert causality on the organic world, it might be a body like those experienced in "out of body" or "near death" experiences, in which the sense organs have shut down even though one can still "see."

The Resurrected Body Will Be in Its Prime

I have often, over the years, thought about these things, especially when confronted with the diminishments of mind and body in friends once bold and strong, or reminded of an infant dying at birth, or faced with my own mother, once a lovely flapper but after 93 years, not at all a flapper or physically lovely when she died. Do any of us want bodies like that? Eternally?

Well, this is Thomas's conjecture in the *Summa Contra Gentiles.* . . . The incorruptible soul, made for the lowly body, bestows on the body something glorious or luminous in its actions, passions and even sufferings. The raised body will be all it was meant to be.

"All must rise," Thomas writes, "in the age of Christ, which is that of youth, by reason of the full flourishing of that nature found at that

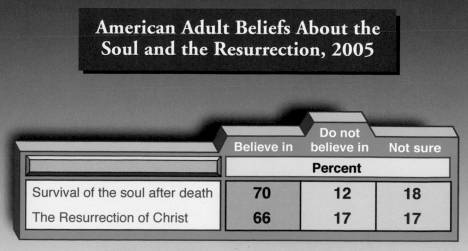

American Adult Beliefs About the Soul and the Resurrection, 2005

	Believe in	Do not believe in	Not sure
		Percent	
Survival of the soul after death	70	12	18
The Resurrection of Christ	66	17	17

Taken from: "The Religious and Other Beliefs of Americans, 2005," Harris Poll No. 90, December 14, 2005. www.harrisinteractive.com.

The empty cross is seen as a symbol of resurrection by many Christians.

age; for the age of childhood has not yet achieved the perfection of what it is, and old age has decreased its ideal perfection.". . .

Our bodies are in effect made glorious: my mother, not that frail filament of a woman, but in her prime; my friend's infant girl-child, not unfinished but fully formed as a person. That child may have no moral wounds to heal, but she will be gloriously human nonetheless.

Older persons, having gone through the crucible of life and choice, joys and sorrows, achievements and diminishments, will re-embody not only all their glories, but all their wounds. These wounds, however, like the risen Lord's, will be glorified.

EVALUATING THE AUTHORS' ARGUMENTS:

In the viewpoint you just read, John F. Kavanaugh contends that after death a person's soul reunites with his or her body. The author of the next viewpoint contends that human beings do not have a soul that survives death. After reading both viewpoints, whose argument do you think is more convincing and why?

There Is No Soul

Alfred Bahr

"We are going to show how absurd the notion of a soul is— that there cannot be a soul."

In the following viewpoint Alfred Bahr contends that the notion of a soul that lives on after death is absurd and impossible. Bahr says Christian and Hindu concepts of the soul are problematic because they do not adequately explain when each person's soul begins or when it ends. Furthermore, Bahr says the Christian idea of a soul, which is based on the teachings of French philosopher René Descartes, is flawed because the spiritual world cannot communicate with the material world. Bahr says there is no soul and there is no life after death.

Alfred Bahr is a physicist and author.

AS YOU READ, CONSIDER THE FOLLOWING QUESTIONS:
1. According to Bahr, when did the Roman Catholic Church admit it was wrong about the teachings of Galileo Galilei?
2. In addition to Hindus, who also believes in a soul that is reborn continuously on Earth, according to the author?
3. Bahr says that, according to Descartes, "consciousness" is located where?

T he question whether we human beings have a soul which survives death is certainly of central importance. Here we are going to investigate what the different religions and especially the Christian church has to say about man and his soul—and also, what the church is now saying after the theory of evolution has appeared and has established itself. Furthermore, we are going to show how absurd the notion of a soul is—that there cannot be a soul. This has, of course, consequences for the belief in a god. If there is no soul and life after death, then there is no 'Beyond' as a domicile for the souls and no god as the creator of the souls.

The Church's Interpretation of Soul After the Theory of Evolution

Before [English naturalist Charles] Darwin published his thesis (*On the Origin of Species,* 1859) that we human beings descended from apes, everyone believed that a god had created man—Adam—according to that god's likeness, some 6,000 years ago out of clay. Afterwards the god injected a soul into that clay figure, which miraculously changed the clay into flesh and blood. Then, from a rib of Adam, Eve was made. This religious fantasy is called 'Creationism' in the USA and is even today taught in the USA in many schools and is really believed by many people to be true.

As Darwin published his thesis, he was immediately attacked and ridiculed by various religious groups. However, the Catholic Church showed surprisingly great restraint. Apparently, it had learned its lesson from the Galileo Affair, and in November 1992 the Roman Catholic Church rehabilitated [Italian astronomer and physicist] Galileo Galilei fully and admitted that the church had been teaching something wrong regarding the motion of the sun. (According to the teaching of the Church, the sun and the stars were circling around the earth, and the earth was the center of the world). The Roman Catholic Church did not want to commit another mistake and was silent as Darwin published his work. Since then, Darwin's theory has been verified many times and finally, in October of 1996, the Pontifical Academy of Science of the Vatican publicly declared the evolution theory of Darwin to be true, with one qualification: The soul of human beings is not the product of evolution but came from 'God.' In this

Darwin's Origin of Species, *outlining evolution, prompted some people to question the existence of a soul.*

manner the church saved its doctrine that 'God' has created mankind. According to the church, human beings without a soul would be just human-looking mindless animals. . . .

The Beginnings and Endings of Souls

Every human being gets a soul at birth. The souls are immortal and continue to live after death. All human beings that ever lived on this planet, but died away after a life-time, continue to live now in the Beyond, forever. The Beyond must therefore be a very crowded place indeed, a place where you can meet any person that ever lived in this world. What a crazy place! . . .

The Christian definition of soul contains a clearly visible logical contradiction. The Christian soul does not have an end in time, but a beginning in time, which is the moment of birth of a human being.

This contradiction is so obvious, that the question comes up, why has the church not given a better definition of the soul? An explanation can be found easily. The church needed desperately a soul which was created by its god. Only in this manner could a human being be made to depend on the grace of the church's god and to pay taxes to the church. If one wanted to remove the beginning in time of the souls, then the souls could not be a creation of a god and the believers would not be bound to that god and the church and would be like the Hindus of India. The Hindus believe that they have a soul which has neither a beginning in time nor an end in time. And in order that this system remain logical, the Hindus believe that the soul is reborn on earth soon after the death of the believer. For completeness sake it should be mentioned here that Pythagoras, the Greek, also believed in a soul which is reborn continuously on earth, and he had many followers.

However, the Indian definition of the soul leads also to contradictions. Namely, from the Indian definition it follows that the number of souls in the world must be constant, since the souls are not created at birth, but existed already. The souls are only reborn souls, never new souls. But if the number of souls is constant, that is, if new souls are never created, then also the number of living creatures, of animals plus men, must at all times be constant. However, we know that this is not the case. There was a time on this planet, when life was impossible. As life developed, we had at first only very few living forms and very few creatures. And as man appeared, we had at first also very few of them. Today the world is overpopulated and close to catastrophe. There is no sign of a constancy of the number of the living creatures and men, and therefore of the number of souls of them. The Indian definition of the soul contradicts reality and must be wrong. In particular, the doctrine that the Indian soul has never been created, but existed always, must be wrong on the ground that everything in this universe had a beginning. . . .

Descartes's Christian Notion of a Soul

Let us now investigate the consequences of the Christian notion of a soul. Descartes (1596–1650), a French Mathematician and Christian Philosopher, taught that the soul is the site of consciousness with a command center. However, the brain perceives, sees, hears, thinks, feels, and remembers. That is, the brain produces the contents of consciousness but reports immediately to the soul what it is seeing, hearing, thinking, etc. The soul, on the other hand, perceives in this manner the outside world and orders the body to move and act. We have a permanent communication between the soul and the brain. According to Descartes this communication is done by means of knocking by the soul on brain cells and by the reverse process, by knocking by brain cells on the soul. This is the central idea of Descartes.

However, it was soon realized that a spiritual soul cannot move material brain cells or knock on material brain cells, and that also the reverse was not possible—namely, that something material can act and knock upon a soul. This means a communication between soul and body is not possible. For this reason the soul of Descartes would not be able to perceive the world, to see and to hear, to think and to remember, etc. The consciousness of this soul would remain without any contents of perception. It would therefore be a black and empty consciousness. . . .

In addition, the body would not be able to receive orders from the soul to move around, and this body would also have no consciousness, because, according to Descartes, the consciousness is located in the soul. But, as we have seen, there is no consciousness in the soul possible, because of the communication problem. However, we know that the body has a consciousness and that the body moves around. This means that consciousness and the command center must be located in the body, and not in the soul. Incidentally, Descartes believed that the existence of 'God' can be proved logically, but did not himself provide such proofs. . . .

No Communication Between the Spiritual and the Material

We are now in a position to draw a very important conclusion, which concerns every god-believer who prays to a god for help. The human being, as a purely material creature, has absolutely no possibility of communicating with a spiritual entity. A communication between something spiritual and material is not possible. This proves that all those Prophets and Apostles like Moses, Paul, and also the Popes in Rome, who also claim to have talked often personally with 'God,' are liars. . . .

The conclusion that there is no life after death possible has, of course, serious consequences regarding the question of gods. If we human beings don't have a soul, and if there is no life after death, then what would a god be good for? What are the regular visits to a church good for? And what is all this talking and preaching of the priest good for? 'God' has no functions to fulfill. He has neither produced souls nor has he created man. Man rather was formed by evolution. This has even been acknowledged by the Roman Catholic Church. And all those people who still believe in a god, who run regularly to church to pray to that god, to ask him for help or to sing the hallelujah, get no rewards for that after death, even if every time they left money behind in the church, or even if they give all their wealth to the church, in order to make the church rich. A life after death they never can buy.

EVALUATING THE AUTHORS' ARGUMENTS:

In the viewpoint you just read, Alfred Bahr asserts that the spiritual soul and the material body cannot communicate with each other. However, the author of the previous viewpoint, John F. Kavanaugh, contends that the body and the soul are reunited in the afterlife. How do you think Kavanaugh would respond to Bahr's contention that the soul and the body cannot communicate?

Facts About Death and Dying

According to the World Health Organization:
- During 2002 an estimated 57 million people died worldwide.
- Nearly 11 million deaths in 2002 were among children under five years of age, and 98 percent of them were in low- and middle-income countries.
- In high-income countries more than two-thirds of all people live beyond the age of seventy and die of chronic diseases: cardiovascular disease, chronic obstructive lung disease, cancers, diabetes or dementia.
- In middle-income countries nearly half of all people live to the age of seventy and chronic diseases are the major killers, just as they are in high-income countries. Unlike in high-income countries, however, HIV/AIDS, complications of pregnancy and childbirth, and road traffic accidents also are leading causes of death.
- In low-income countries less than a quarter of all people reach the age of seventy, and nearly a third of all deaths are among children under fourteen. Complications of pregnancy and childbirth together continue to be a leading cause of death, claiming the lives of both infants and mothers.
- Cardiovascular diseases kill more people each year—in high-, middle-, and low-income countries alike—than any others. In 2002, 7.2 million people died of coronary heart disease, 5.5 million from stroke or another form of cerebrovascular disease.

According to the U.S. Centers for Disease Control and Prevention, National Center for Health Statistics:
- In 2004 a total of 2.4 million deaths occurred in the United States.
- The fifteen leading causes of death in the United States in 2004 were:
  - Heart disease (27.2 percent)
  - Cancer (23.1 percent)
  - Stroke (6.3 percent)
  - Chronic lower respiratory diseases (5.1 percent)

- Accidents (4.7 percent)
- Diabetes (3.1 percent)
- Alzheimer's disease (2.8 percent)
- Influenza and pneumonia (2.5 percent)
- Kidney disease (1.8 percent)
- Septicemia (1.4 percent)
- Suicide (1.4 percent)
- Chronic liver disease and cirrhosis (1.1 percent)
- Hypertension (1 percent)
- Parkinson's disease (0.8 percent)
- Homicide (0.7 percent)

Average Life Expectancy in the United States in 2004
- Men, all races   75.2 years
- Women, all races   80.4 years
- Men, white   75.7 years
- Men, black   69.5 years
- Women, white   80.8 years
- Women, black   76.3 years

Average Human Life Expectancy Throughout History
- Prehistoric times   18 years of age
- Ancient Greece   20 years of age
- Middle Ages (England)   33 years of age
- 1620, Massachusetts Bay Colony   35 years of age
- Nineteenth-century England   41 years of age
- 1900, United States   47 years of age
- 1915, United States   54 years of age
- 1950, United States   68 years of age
- 2000, United States   77 years of age
- 2004, United States   77.8 years of age

Maximum Recorded Life Spans for Different Species
- Bivalve mollusks   405–410 years
- Whales   210 years
- Galapagos turtle   190 years
- Humans   122.4 years
- Elephants   78 years

- Chimpanzees   75 years
- Horses   62 years
- Goldfish   49 years
- Cats   36 years
- Dogs   29 years
- Mice   4 years

According to the National Hospice and Palliative Care Organization, the number of patients served by hospice in the United States was:

- 495,000 in 1997
- 540,000 in 1998
- 620,000 in 1999
- 700,000 in 2000
- 775,000 in 2001
- 885,000 in 2002
- 950,000 in 2003
- 1,060,000 in 2004
- 1,200,000 in 2005
- 1,300,000 in 2006

Organizations to Contact

The editors have compiled the following list of organizations concerned with the issues debated in this book. The descriptions are derived from materials provided by the organizations. All have publications or information available for interested readers. The list was compiled on the date of publication of the present volume; the information provided here may change. Be aware that many organizations take several weeks or longer to respond to inquiries, so allow as much time as possible.

American Society for Law, Medicine, and Ethics (ASLME)
765 Commonwealth Ave., Suite 1634, Boston, MA 02215
(617) 262-4990
fax: (617) 437-7596
e-mail: info@aslme.org
Web site: www.aslme.org

The ASLME provides educational information at the intersection of law, medicine, and ethics. The organization focuses on research projects on undertreating pain and end-of-life issues. The ASLME publishes two quarterly journals, the *Journal of Law, Medicine & Ethics* and the *American Journal of Law & Medicine.*

Association for Death Education and Counseling (ADEC)
60 Revere Dr., Suite 500, Northbrook, IL 60062
(847) 509-0403
fax: (847) 480-9282
e-mail: www.adec.org/contact.cfm
Web site: www.adec.org

The ADEC is an interdisciplinary organization that provides education and support in the fields of dying, death, and bereavement. The ADEC offers numerous educational conferences, courses, and workshops, and it publishes a newsletter called the *Forum.*

Atheist Alliance International (AAI)
PO Box 242, Pocopson, PA 19366
(866) 437-3842

e-mail: info@atheistalliance.org
Web site: www.atheistalliance.org

AAI promotes independent religion and atheistic societies. The alliance believes there is no evidence of reincarnation of the human soul. It provides education and information about atheism and rational thinking. The organization publishes *Secular Nation*, a quarterly magazine, and the *Journal of Higher Criticism*, a publication of biblical study.

Center for Bioethics and Human Dignity

Trinity International University, 2065 Half Day Rd., Deerfield, IL 60015
(847) 317-8180
fax: (847) 317-8101
e-mail: info@cbhd.org
Web site: www.cbhd.org

The Center for Bioethics and Human Dignity is a nonprofit organization that seeks to bring the Christian viewpoint to bioethical issues such as those that surround end-of-life care. The center produces a wide range of live, recorded, and written resources examining bioethical issues. The center's Web site offers overviews, bibliographies, and case studies on major bioethical issues such as death and dying.

Center for Thanatology Research and Education

391 Atlantic Ave., Brooklyn, NY 11217-1701
(718) 858-3026
fax: (718) 852-1846
e-mail: thanatology@pipeline.com
Web site: www.thanatology.org

The Center for Thanatology Research and Education is a nonprofit library, museum, and resource center for all topics dealing with death. The organization also publishes books and periodicals about death, such as *Advances in Thanatology, Journals of the Foundation of Thanatology*, and the *Thanatology News*.

Centering Corporation

7230 Maple St., Omaha, NE 68134
(866) 218-0101

e-mail: www.centeringcorp.com/catalog/contact_us.php
Web site: www.centeringcorp.com

The Centering Corporation is a nonprofit organization dedicated to providing education and resources for the bereaved. The organization provides educational offerings and workshops for caregivers and families. It publishes the *Grief Digest*, a quarterly magazine supporting grieving people and caregivers; *Fire in My Heart*, a journal for teenagers experiencing a loss; and *I Remember, I Remember*, a journal for adults experiencing a loss.

Compassion and Choices
PO Box 101810, Denver, CO 80250-1810
(800) 247-7421
fax: (303) 639-1224
e-mail: info@compassionandchoices.org
Web site: www.compassionandchoices.org

Compassion and Choices is a nonprofit organization working to legalize physician-assisted suicide and improve end-of-life care. Compassion and Choices was originally founded as the Hemlock Society in 1980. The organization seeks to change U.S. laws to expand choice at the end of life. It publishes the quarterly *Compassion and Choices* magazine.

Death with Dignity National Center (DDNC)
520 SW Sixth Ave., Suite 1030, Portland, OR 97204
(503) 228-4415
fax: (503) 228-7454
e-mail: www.deathwithdignity.org/whatwedo/contact.asp
Web site: www.deathwithdignity.org

The DDNC is a nonprofit organization that works to defend the Oregon Death with Dignity law and promote choice in end-of-life decisions. The group leads the legal defense of the Death with Dignity law and provides education and outreach. Various editorials and personal stories are published on the group's Web site.

Hastings Center
21 Malcolm Gordon Rd., Garrison, NY 10524-4125
(845) 424-4040

fax: (845) 424-4545
e-mail: mail@thehastingscenter.org
Web site: www.thehastingscenter.org

The Hastings Center is an independent, nonpartisan, and nonprofit bioethics research institute founded in 1969 to explore fundamental and emerging questions in medicine, health care, and biotechnology. One of the center's main areas of research is in the area of decision making at the end of life. The organization publishes two bimonthly journals, the *Hastings Center Report* and *IRB: Ethics and Human Research*.

Hospice Foundation of America
1621 Connecticut Ave. NW, Suite 300, Washington, DC 20009
(800) 854-3402
fax: (202) 638-5312
e-mail: hfaoffice@hospicefoundation.org
Web site: www.hospicefoundation.org

The Hospice Foundation of America is a nonprofit organization that seeks to enhance the role of hospice in the American health-care system. The foundation conducts programs of professional development, provides public education and information, and facilitates research into hospice and other health-care issues. They sponsor the Annual Bereavement Teleconference on Grief Issues and produce a monthly newsletter called *Journeys*, which features articles to help the bereaved.

International Association for Near-Death Studies (IANDS)
PO Box 50, East Windsor Hill, CT 06028
(860) 882-1211
fax: (860) 882-1212
e-mail: www.iands.org/contact.html#email
Web site: www.iands.org

The IANDS is the only organization in the world devoted exclusively to the study of near-death experiences (NDEs) and near-deathlike experiences. Its mission is to build global understanding of NDEs through research, education, and support. The organization publishes the periodic *Journal of Near-Death Studies*, a quarterly newsletter called *Vital Signs*, and various informational brochures.

International Task Force on Euthanasia and Assisted Suicide

PO Box 760, Steubenville, OH 43952

(740) 282-3810

e-mail: www.internationaltaskforce.org/comments.htm

Web site: www.internationaltaskforce.org

The International Task Force on Euthanasia and Assisted Suicide is a nonprofit organization that opposes physician-assisted suicide and euthanasia. The organization seeks to influence public policy and educate people about the dangers of physician-assisted suicide and euthanasia. It publishes a periodic newsmagazine called the *Update*.

The Monroe Institute

365 Roberts Mountain Rd., Faber, VA 22938

(866) 881-3440

fax: (434) 361-1237

e-mail: monroeinst@aol.com

Web site: www.monroeinstitute.com

The Monroe Institute is a nonprofit education and research organization devoted to the exploration of human consciousness. The institute is devoted to the premise that focused consciousness contains definitive solutions to the major issues of human experience. The institute publishes the *Hemi-Sync® Journal*, a periodic research and educational journal, and the newsletter *TMI Focus*, as well as offering many videotapes and multimedia resources.

National Catholic Ministry to the Bereaved (NCMB)

PO Box 16353, St. Louis, MO 63125-0353

(314) 638-2638

fax: (314) 638-2639

e-mail: ncmb@griefwork.org

Web site: www.griefwork.org

The NCMB offers pastoral and spiritual support based on Christian beliefs to people of all faiths who have suffered the loss of a loved one. The organization develops and provides resources and training programs to religious grief counselors, parishes, and dioceses. The NCMB sponsors an annual conference and also publishes a quarterly newsletter, *Journey*, as well as several brochures and pamphlets about grief.

National Funeral Directors Association (NFDA)
13625 Bishop's Dr., Brookfield, WI 53005
(800) 228-6332
fax: (262) 789-6977
e-mail: nfda@nfda.org
Web site: www.nfda.org

The NFDA is a worldwide resource and advocate for the funeral service industry and helps the industry to provide ethical and meaningful services to the public. The organization provides education and information about funeral services to the public as well as to the funeral services industry. The NFDA produces a periodical called the *Director* as well as the *NFDA Bulletin.*

The Skeptics Society
PO Box 338, Altadena, CA 91001
(626) 794-3119
fax: (626) 794-1301
e-mail: skepticssociety@skeptic.com
Web site: www.skeptic.com

The Skeptics Society is a scientific and educational organization that serves as an educational tool for those seeking clarification and viewpoints on controversial ideas and claims. The society engages in scientific investigation and journalistic research to investigate claims made by scientists, historians, and controversial figures on a wide range of subjects, including religion and life after death. The Skeptics Society produces a quarterly magazine called *Skeptic.*

For Further Reading

Books

Margaret Pabst Battin, *Ending Life: Ethics and the Way We Die.* Oxford, UK: Oxford University Press, 2005. This book covers a wide range of end-of-life topics, including suicide prevention, AIDS, suicide bombing, serpent handling, and other religious practices that pose a risk of death or suicide.

Pauline W. Chen, *Final Exam: A Surgeon's Reflections on Mortality.* New York: Alfred A. Knopf, 2007. Chen recounts her immediate experience with dying and dead persons and what she learned from it, including the need for greater empathy in end-of-life care.

Deepak Chopra, *Life After Death: The Burden of Proof.* New York: Harmony, 2006. Chopra, a medical doctor and world leader in mind-body medicine, attempts to answer what happens after we die. Chopra believes there is life after death.

Lisa Takeuchi Cullen, *Remember Me: A Lively Tour of the New American Way of Death.* New York: HarperCollins, 2006. A survey of American funeral customs. It explores the innumerable ways in which funerals are being personalized, publicized, economized, commercialized, and trivialized.

Ian Rober Dowbiggin, *A Merciful End: The Euthanasia Movement in Modern America.* Oxford, UK: Oxford University Press, 2003. This work provides an objective presentation and study of euthanasia.

John Edward, *After Life: Answers from the Other Side.* New York: Princess, 2003. Psychic medium Edward answers questions about life after death and how mediums work.

Norman J. Fried, *The Angel Letters: Lessons That Dying Can Teach Us About Living.* Chicago: Ivan R. Dee, 2007. Fried, a child psychologist who has worked with pediatric oncology patients, writes letters to children who have died from cancer. He conveys a sense of each child's struggle in each letter.

Sandra M. Gilbert, *Death's Door: Modern Dying and the Ways We Grieve*. New York: W.W. Norton, 2006. This book looks at death across time and culture: in the Nazi concentration camps, 9/11, and the twenty-first-century "hospital spaceship," as well as through photographs, paintings, and poetry.

Karm-glin-pa, Padma Sambhava, and Gyurme Dorje, *The Tibetan Book of the Dead*. New York: Viking, 2006. This work contains guidance on how to address the process of dying in the after-death states and on how to help those who are dying.

Robert Kastenbaum, *On Our Way: The Final Passage Through Life and Death*. Berkeley and Los Angeles: University of California Press, 2004. This is a survey of religious beliefs and practices from a variety of cultures.

Stephen P. Kiernan, *Last Rights: Rescuing the End of Life from the Medical System*. New York: St. Martin's, 2006. Kiernan discusses how medical advances have changed the way people die and reveals a disconnect between how people want to die and how the medical system treats the dying.

Neal Nicol and Harry Wilie, *Between the Dying and the Dead: Dr. Jack Kevorkian's Life and the Battle to Legalize Euthanasia*. Madison: University of Wisconsin Press, 2006. An interview with Jack Kevorkian, known as Dr. Death, who was imprisoned for assisting over a hundred people to die in the 1990s.

Arthur O. Roberts, *Exploring Heaven: What Great Christian Thinkers Tell Us About Our Afterlife with God*. HarperSanFranciso: 2003. Using religious teachings, scientific knowledge, and biblical insights, Roberts addresses elusive questions, such as where is heaven located? What exactly is eternal life? And who inhabits heaven?

Periodicals

Jonathan Aitken, "Let's Talk About Death," *American Spectator*, 2007.

K.J. Bishop, "The Art of Dying," *Boston Review*, September/October 2007.

William Blazek, "A White on White Whiteness," *Washington Post*, October 16, 2007.

Sarah Blustain, "No Country for Mothers," *American Prospect*, October 2007.

Jane Brody, "A Doctor's Duty, When Death Is Inevitable," *New York Times*, August 10, 2004.

Janet L. Factor, "The Gift of a Wise Man (Accepting One's Mortality)," *Free Inquiry*, October/November 2007.

Kathleen M. Foley, "Is Physician-Assisted Suicide Ever Acceptable? It's Never Acceptable," *Family Practice News*, June 1, 2007.

Gail Gazelle, "Understanding Hospice—an Underutilized Option for Life's Final Chapter," *New England Journal of Medicine*, July 26, 2007.

John Gillman, "Death and the Afterlife in the New Testament," *Catholic Biblical Quarterly*, 2007.

Leor Halevi, "The Torture of the Grave: Islam and the Afterlife," *International Herald Tribune*, May 4, 2007.

Molly McHugh, "Physician-Assisted Suicide Is the More Humane Option," *Salem* [OR] *Statesman Journal*, August 28, 2008.

Steven Moffic, "Dr. Death and the Meaning of Life," *Clinical Psychiatry News*, September 2007.

Michael Petrou, "A Time to Die: Is the Dutch Model of Euthanasia—Even for Infants—the Solution When Suffering Can't be Relieved?" *Maclean's*, September 5, 2005.

Robert Pollack, "Attending to the Pain of the Dying: An Agenda for Science," *Cross Currents*, Summer 2006.

Timothy E. Quill, "Is Physician-Assisted Suicide Ever Acceptable? It's Justified in Rare Cases," *Family Practice News*, June 1, 2007.

Nancy Rommelmann, "Crying and Digging: Reclaiming the Realities and Rituals of Death," *Los Angeles Times*, February 6, 2005.

Ann V. Shibler, "Defying the Death Culture," *New American*, May 16, 2005.

Sidney Wanzer, "The Dying of the Light," *New Scientist*, March 24, 2007.

Internet Sources

Joanne Kenen, "In Search of a Gentler End," Stateline.org, October 29, 2007. www.stateline.org/live/details/story?contendID=252525.

Steve Pavlina, "Life After Death," 2005. www.stevepavlina.com/articles/life-after-death.htm.

Lesley Williams, "Dealing with Death and Dying," Ezine Articles, April 8, 2007. www.ezinearticles.com/?Dealing-With-Death-and-Dying&id=518928.

Web Sites

All About GOD (www.allaboutgod.com). This site is hosted by an evangelical Christian group that attempts to reach out to skeptics, seekers, and believers with evidence for the existence of God and Jesus.

Growth House (www.growthhouse.org). A resource portal for life-threatening illnesses and end-of-life care. It explains major issues in hospice and home care, palliative care, pain management, grief, and death with dignity.

Hospice Net (www.hospicenet.org). This site provides comprehensive resources to anyone interested in hospice.

International Survivalist Society (www.survivalafterdeath.org). This Web site publishes articles, books, and photographs relating to survival after death and psychical research.

Kill the Afterlife (http://killtheafterlife.blogspot.com). This site provides resources that denounce the concept of life after death, believing this concept is inhumane and immoral.

Near-Death Experiences and the Afterlife (http://near-death.com). This Web site profiles the most profound near-death experiences ever documented, along with supporting scientific, metaphysical, and religious material.

Origins (www.origins.org). This site features scholarly and popular resources concerning intelligent design and philosophical theism.

Religious Tolerance (www.religioustolerance.org). This site describes both the positive and negative aspects of religions and describes dozens of faith groups and all sides of controversial topics, including physician-assisted suicide.

Index

Niacin, 43
Nicodemus, 73, 75, 80
Nutritional supplements, 43

O
On Death and Dying (Kübler-Ross), 8
On the Origin of Species (Darwin), 105–106
Oregon Death with Dignity Act, 48, 53
Origen, 72
Out-of-body experiences (OBEs), 95–97
See also Near-death experiences (NDEs)

P
Panzer, Ron, 63
Paradise, 86
Paranormal beliefs, 93
Parkes, Collin Murray, 8
Partnership for Caring, 66
Paul, Margaret, 25
Persinger, Michael, 96
Physician-assisted suicide (PAS)
persons with disabilities and, 55–56
public opinion on, 50
should be legal, 47–51, 65
should not be allowed, 52–57
Physicians. *See* Doctors
Plants, souls of, 99
Preston, Tom, 47
Priest, role of, 12

Q
Quality of life, 45, 59–60
Quantum machines, 88–90

Quinlan, Karen Ann, 55

R
Rabbi, 12
Rebirth. *See* Reincarnation
Reflexive consciousness, 99–100
Reincarnation
Hinduism and, 107
is in the Bible, 70–76
is not in Bible, 77–83
karma and, 86
misconceptions about, 71
public belief in, 75, 79
Religion
can devalue life, 31–35
can ease grief over death, 11–17
corrupts death, 18–24
death process and, 15–17
fear of death and, 19–20, 26–27
learning to believe in, 29–30
Religious leaders
fear of death and, 19–20
role of, 12–14, 17
Religious syncretism, 78
Resurrection
of body, 72–73, 98–103
misunderstanding over, 71–72
spiritual, 72, 75, 76, 80–82
Right to die movement, 64
Rishis, 94
Rituals
funeral, 12–17, 20–22
mourning, 14–15
Roman Catholic Church. *See* Catholic Church

Picture Credits

Cover photo: Image copyright James Steidl, 2007. Used under license from Shutterstock.com

Maury Aaseng, 16, 21, 27, 34, 38, 42, 50, 61, 67, 79, 89, 96, 101

Image copyright Nick Alexander, 2008. Used under license from Shutterstock.com, 95

AP Images, 33, 44, 48, 54, 59, 65, 81

Shaun Curry/AFP/Getty, 106

Image copyright EML, 2008. Used under license from Shutterstock.com, 69

Image copyright Flashon Studio, 2008. Used under license from Shutterstock.com, 102

Rich Frishman/Time Life Pictures/Getty Images, 85

Getty Images News, 29

Image copyright Keith McIntyre, 2008. Used under license from Shutterstock.com, 74

Jill Nance-Pool/Getty Images, 23

Joe Radele/Getty Images, 13

Jan Sonnenmair/Aurora/Getty Images, 39

Image copyright Fara Spence, 2008. Used under license from Shutterstock.com, 10

Jim West/Alamy, 46